SINGING THE LORD'S SONG
IN A NEW LAND

SINGING THE LORD'S SONG IN A NEW LAND

Korean American Practices of Faith

Su Yon Pak, Unzu Lee, Jung Ha Kim,
and Myung Ji Cho

WESTMINSTER
JOHN KNOX PRESS
LOUISVILLE • KENTUCKY

Scripture quotations from the New Revised Standard Version of the Bible are copyright © 1989 by the Division of Christian Education of the National Council of the Churches of Christ in the U.S.A. and are used by permission.

Scripture quotations from the Revised Standard Version of the Bible are copyright © 1946, 1952, 1971, and 1973 by the Division of Christian Education of the National Council of the Churches of Christ in the U.S.A. and are used by permission.

Chapter 1 is a revision of the previously published work, along with reprints of sections from Jung Ha Kim's "Cartography of Korean American Protestant Faith Communities in the United States," in *Religions in Asian America: Building Faith Communities*, ed. Pyong Gap Min and Jung Ha Kim (Walnut Creek, Calif.: AltaMira Press, 2002). Used by permission of Rowman & Littlefield Publishing Group.

Book design by Sharon Adams
Cover design by Night & Day Design

First edition
Published by Westminster John Knox Press
Louisville, Kentucky

This book is printed on acid-free paper that meets the American National Standards Institute Z39.48 standard. ∞

PRINTED IN THE UNITED STATES OF AMERICA

05 06 07 08 09 10 11 12 13 14 — 10 9 8 7 6 5 4 3 2 1

Library of Congress Cataloging-in-Publication Data

Singing the Lord's song in a new land : Korean American practices of faith /
Su Yon Pak . . . [et al.].
     p. cm.
  Includes bibliographical references.
  ISBN 0-664-22878-X (alk. paper)
  1. Korean Americans—Religion. I. Pak, Su Yon.

BR563.K67S55 2005
277.3'082'08957—dc22   2004058589

For our mothers—

Choi Soo Jin
Kim In Ock
Kim Yang Sook
Noh Yung Soon

And our daughters—

Grace
Elizabeth
Seri
Mina

Contents

Foreword

Across the ages Christian communities have expressed and embodied their faith in an inconceivable variety of cultural settings. The meals Christians have shared with strangers and one another have included the produce of every land and the spice of every cuisine. Praying and singing, Christians have articulated lament and praise in a multitude of tongues. Offering care to those who are sick or dying, Christians have imbued the healing arts of many nations with the love of Christ. Throughout the world, in these everyday acts and many more, they have responded in a host of accents to God's grace in Christ through their participation in practices that address human needs and reflect the love of God.

One faith unites these many and diverse incarnations of Christian practice. At the same time, each is distinctive because it is shaped by the cultural setting within which it takes on flesh. The incarnational quality of Christian faith offers to each Christian community the joy and the difficulty of working out the specific forms that practices will take within each community's historical and cultural particularity. Much of this work takes place implicitly, as Christians adapt practices to their own language and circumstance through the negotiations of daily living. But explicit reflection is also important, for it provides crucial opportunities for retrieving, appreciating, criticizing, and strengthening practices.

Singing the Lord's Song in a New Land gives voice to a distinctive incarnation of Christian faith and life—that of the Korean American Christian community, especially as this is experienced by women. (Actually, we soon learn, this community also embraces considerable diversity within itself.) By focusing on the meaning and lived reality of its central practices, the four authors offer readers deep insight into a vibrant community in the midst of a complex process of negotiating among Korean, American, and Christian influences on the patterns of daily life, patterns that are complicated by generation and gender as well.

I am delighted that these thoughtful and committed authors have found the idea of practices developed by my colleagues and me in *Practicing Our Faith* helpful in their work. Focusing on practices, they affirm, has helped them to understand important patterns and challenges within their community. It is my earnest hope that this book will make such understanding available to other Korean Americans, as well as to those from other cultural backgrounds who are their brothers and sisters in faith. Most of all, I hope that whatever understanding is gained will be a source of wisdom and strength as the Korean American Christian community and other communities seek to grow more faithful in the practices that shape our lives as Christians.

The cultural diversity of Christianity is especially evident in this twenty-first century of the life of the Church. In this period of global change and increased communication, travel, and migration, the international and multicultural character of Christian faith can be seen not only on the world map but also in every city of North America. Coming to recognize and learn from this diversity is among the most important theological and educational tasks facing contemporary Christians, no matter what their own cultural ground might be. I am grateful to Dr. Su Yon Pak, Dr. Jung Ha Kim, Dr. Unzu Lee, and Rev. Myung Ji Cho for their fine contribution to this crucial work of the church in our time.

Dorothy C. Bass

Acknowledgments

This project is the work of many hands. We are especially grateful for generous funding from the Valparaiso Project, which enabled us to collaborate effectively on this project. Special appreciation goes to Dorothy Bass and Don Richter, who believed in the importance of this work for the Korean American community. Their recognition was a great encouragement for us. We would also like to thank the Center for Pan Asian Community Services, Inc. in Atlanta for providing institutional support and managing the funds. Our sincere appreciation goes to Jon L. Berquist, the Senior Academic Editor at Westminster John Knox Press, for his interest and commitment and for taking a leap of faith in engaging this project.

Personally, Su Yon Pak would like to thank Kathy Talvacchia for her unending support and for her thorough proofreading and editing. Heartfelt gratitude goes to her Korean American faith communities in New York City, who first claimed her as their daughter and without whom her faith journey would have been incomplete.

Unzu Lee wishes to thank her mother, Noh Yung Soon, for allowing her to practice freedom throughout her faith journey in her search for truth. Also, she is grateful to the Korean immigrant churches that not only provided nurture and community but taught her how she should live out her faith as a Korean American woman in this strange land.

Jung Ha Kim would like to thank Chaiwon Kim, "Johnnie's mother," "Swannee's mother," "Michelle's mother," and other women adherents of the Korean American Church of Atlanta, UMC for sharing their everyday journeys of faith. "Thank you, Jenny Jeung, Annie Kim, Heather and Nahna Kim, Mina and Emily Yi, and Minnie Lee for including me as an honorary member of the baby-buster generation." The Department of Sociology at Georgia State University also deserves a word of thanks for providing the optimal collegial atmosphere to work and for many long-lasting friendships.

Myung Ji Cho would like to acknowledge her late older sister, Cho Young Ock, whose ideals and dreams of women's freedom and liberation were realized in her own life. Young Ock's grief for her unfulfilled dream as well as the silent, yet tender song in her heart were always revealed in her artistic drawing.

Finally, we are grateful for each other and for our commitment and tenacity to build and sustain this relationship. Our friendship enabled four very different Korean American women to work and grow together, both individually and as a group. For this, we know that we are truly blessed.

Introduction

How do Korean American Christians practice their faith? Many communities throughout generations have participated in Christian practices not only as a way to embody faith but perhaps more fundamentally to come to faith. Why? Christian practices are activities Christian people do together over time. They constitute a way of life that is lived out in a world "created and sustained by a just and merciful God, who is now in the midst of reconciling this world through Christ."[1] They address fundamental human needs in ways that reflect God's purpose for humankind. Although these human needs—the need for healing, for community, to be fed and cared for, for instance—are fundamental and universal for every living human being, differing historical, political, racial, economic, cultural, and social contexts create different and particular ways in which these needs are met. Also, certain needs are more urgent and prominent in one community than in others. For Korean American Christians, practicing their faith gives structure to the chaos caused by many generations of turmoil on Korean soil, and by the effects of immigration to the United States, such as cultural, political, and economic discontinuities; discrimination;

and generational conflicts. Practicing faith gives meaning in the midst of apparent meaninglessness.

Given the critical role that practices play in Korean American faith communities, the following questions can be raised: How do Korean American Christians practice their faith? What do they practice? What are some "Western/ American" practices that Korean Americans have adopted and adapted? What are some indigenous practices that Korean Americans have drawn upon? How does immigration affect Christian practices and vice versa? What happens to practices that no longer fit? What about "broken" practices? What happens to the community when these practices are no longer preserved and practiced, as in the case of second- and subsequent-generation Korean Americans? How are these practices passed on from generation to generation?

These are the guiding questions for this work, which highlights practices that are both particular and essential to Korean American Christians. As Korean Americans celebrate the centennial anniversary of immigration and community building in the United States (1903–2003), the foregoing questions also provide opportunities for reflecting on the past and envisioning the future. Drawing on the twelve practices[2] found in Dorothy Bass's book *Practicing Our Faith*, this book identifies eight Christian practices that are essential in the Korean American context. Although these eight practices do not neatly fit into the framework that Bass articulates, beginning from our cultural particularity allows us to be in conversation with and challenge her categories while at the same time exploring the richness of our own heritage. This expands the notion of Christian practices into a more inclusive reality that embraces the global nature of Christian practices. Thus, rather than asking *how* Korean Americans participate in a specific practice, such as singing, we ask first, *what* practices are essential to Korean American Protestants. From a point of first understanding what is essential to us as Korean Americans, we then reflect on the *ways* that these practices influence aspects of our lives.

As we began this work, we first thought primarily of second- and subsequent-generation Korean Americans as our intended audience. As four immigrant women who have experienced multiple immigrations (one came to the United States via Japan; another, via Brazil; another has lived in the Philippines; another, in Scotland) and have lived in the United States for a major part of our lives, we are in the position of being immersed in this community of practice while at the same time having critical distance from it. As we came together for more focused conversations and further probing, our intended audience also became more inclusive and open. We write this book with a passion to converse with subsequent generations and other communities of practicing faith about why we do what we do. It is intended to enhance intergenerational and cross-cultural bridge building. If we can participate in some of these practices together, or even understand why a particular generation practices their faith in a certain way, we can begin to overcome some of the existing alienation between generations and cultures. This book is a letter or a conversation with our daughters, sons, and neighbors. Others outside the Christian context who wish to learn about Korean American Protestant practices can join in the conversation, understanding that we are speaking primarily about our own community of faith practices.

The format of the book is as follows: The first part sets the context with a brief overview of the history of the Korean American church in the United States. The second part contains eight chapters that embody the specific practices to be discussed. "This Is the Day" discusses Korean American experiences of observing Sabbath, participating in early morning prayer, and honoring the body. "Let Everything That Has Breath, Sing!" addresses the importance of singing for Korean Americans as a practice of forming individual and communal identities. It creates a sense of belonging and rootedness. "Fervent Prayer" introduces as a unique Korean practice of faith *tong-sung ki-do,* which literally means "praying together out loud." It also touches on practices of discernment and testimony. "Resourcing the Life Circle" articulates a Korean American perspective on living and dying well. "Bearing Wisdom" explores how the valuing of wisdom shapes community and discernment. "Gathering at the Well" uses the metaphor of "well-digging" to illustrate the dynamic between building up and breaking down community and to examine the schismatic tendency of the Korean American church. "Thy Will Be Done" discusses prayer in fasting as a practice done for specific liturgical seasons as well as for individuals and groups. "'Ricing' Community" discusses the practice of mutual nurturing through sharing of resources within the community.

Each chapter discusses the practice—what it is, how it is practiced and why, and how it can be improved. Although many of these practices originated from Korea, the context and the focus of these chapters are Korean American. At the end of each chapter are questions for discussion that take readers more deeply into not only Korean American practices but also their own. They are questions that invite readers to think critically about practices and about how and what they teach the way people live their lives. Bass and Dykstra speak of practices as "rehearsing a way of life."[3] These questions are intended to draw attention to how readers rehearse their ways of life.

This book is designed so that readers can choose to study all eight practices consecutively or to study selected ones of interest. They will also find some repetition and overlap of information from chapter to chapter. We wrote it this way for three reasons: First, in order for each chapter to stand on its own, sufficient information needs to be given to contextualize the practice. Second, pedagogically, repetition can help educate, especially if the content is new to readers. For example, we mention Confucian ideology in several chapters not only because it has a tremendous impact on Korean American lives but also because repetition helps the reader understand what might be a new worldview. Third, in reality practices actually do overlap and repeat. Singing our lives can be a part of dying well as well as keeping Sabbath. Repetition, a critical element of any practice, also reflects the way we live out our lives in practice. We rehearse a way of life.

The writers of this group, Resource and Information Center for Empowerment (RICE), come from varied backgrounds, but all possess a similar passion to work on projects relevant to Korean/Asian American communities. Rev. Myung Ji Cho is currently an Associate Pastor of English Language Ministry (ELM) at the Korean United Methodist Church of South Suburban Chicago. She has served a predominantly African American UMC congregation in Chicago and two Anglo UMC congregations in Ohio, and has also worked as a hospital chaplain. Rev. Dr. Unzu Lee, an ordained minister in the Presbyterian Church (U.S.A.), is Associate for Presbyterian Women Leadership Development, PC(USA), and has also served as Coordinator for Women's Advocacy in the PC(USA) General Assembly Office, Louisville. She is a long-term advocate for racial and gender justice. Dr. Jung Ha Kim is a Senior Lecturer of Sociology at Georgia State University. She also devotes much of her spare time serving/managing the Asian American Community Center in Atlanta. She is the author of *Bridge-makers and Cross-bearers* (1997), along with numerous other published articles and chapters, and the co-editor of *Religions in Asian America* (2002). She currently serves as co-chair for the Women and Religion Section of the American Academy of Religion. Dr. Su Yon Pak is the Associate Dean for Student Life and Director of Recruitment at Union Theological Seminary in New York City. She teaches education courses on family/community and im/migration and education at Teachers College, Columbia University and has written for the United Church Press's young adult curriculum *Push It!* She currently serves as co-chair for the Asian North American Religion, Culture, and Society Group of the American Academy of Religion. Together as a group, RICE has already published a Bible study in Korean for Korean American women: *Searching for Home in the Bible: Home is the Place Where Our Stories Are Told* (Nashville: United Methodist Publishing House, 1999), which links together biblical stories, early immigrants' stories (from the early 1900s), and contemporary Korean American women's stories.

One word to note about the written style of this text: This work was a true collaborative effort and the writing styles and thought processes that each of us employed became naturally incorporated into the text as a whole. Our process for this project included an initial articulation of our own faith practices from our families and faith communities. From there, we discerned what were, in our opinion, the most common and unique practices of our community. Together, we constructed the components of each practice as well as concepts and directions to be explored in each of the chapters. We were all assigned various chapters to author, which then were subjected to our collaborative scrutiny. Even the final revisions were a collaborative process. As a result, the text may at times reflect the various voices and the writing styles of our authors, which we have intentionally chosen to leave intact as an expression of the diversity of our community. Similarly, the text embodies this dynamism in the way that we refer to the Korean American community: in some instances that relationship is expressed as "we" and others as "they." This reveals our standpoint as simultaneous members of the community and observers of the community's practice.

Finally, this book is not the definitive word on how and why Korean Americans practice the way they do. Our intention is to begin a conversation by articulating something that has not yet been articulated. Our perspective is predominantly Protestant, more specifically, Presbyterian and Methodist Christianity. We found that even among ourselves there were differing practices and differences of opinions. Sometimes we found ourselves vehemently disagreeing with each other while at the same time recognizing that there is not one way to practice Korean American Protestant faith. Even among the four of us, we had alliances along certain lines: denomination, age, class, year of immigration (how long we've been in the United States); regional (east coast, west coast, north, or south; and whether our original home—before the 38th parallel division—was in northern or southern Korea); clergy/laity; family of origin and tradition. We found ourselves shifting alliances depending on the issue, sometimes two against two, and other times, three against one (!). We shared painful stories as well as stories of joy and humor. We ate and laughed a lot. But what became clear was that negotiating our way through our own understandings of practices was itself an enriching and bonding experience. And as the readers join us in our conversation, we welcome stories of differing experiences, opinions, and memories of "ritual genesis."[4] This book is an invitation to such conversations.

Chapter 1

A Social History of the Korean American Church in the United States[1]

Raymond Brady Williams, a historian of religion, asserts that "American society presents a moving kaleidoscope of living religions through which one can observe both the evolving shapes of American religion and the religious histories that all immigrants are contributing to the American history."[2] Among these vibrant actors who precipitate rapid changes in American religion, and, more specifically, Christianity, are Korean Americans. An estimated 70 to 75 percent of one million Korean Americans living in the United States are gathered into over three thousand of their own ethnic churches every Sunday. This also means that there is roughly one ethnic church for every 330 Korean Americans. As Stephen Warner observed, "Korean Americans are so well organized religiously and so reflective about their religious experiences in the United States that they offer the student of American religion an ideal opportunity to explore the parameters of recent change."[3] Indeed, "Korean Americans have been at the forefront of immigrant groups in coming to scholarly grips with their own religious experiences."[4]

While the numerical growth of the Korean American church has generated studies documenting its schismatic tendencies, the relatively small size of

Korean American local congregations, the conflict between the Korean-speaking congregation (KSC) and the English-speaking congregation (ESC) along generational lines, and gendered experiences in the church, very little attention has been given to examining the practiced religion within the Korean American church.[5] The practiced religion as the very embodiment of Christian faith has been defined as "things Christian people do together over time to address fundamental needs in response to and in light of God's active presence for the life of the world."[6] As such, scholars of congregational studies point to the practiced religion as the "culture of congregation." Nancy T. Ammerman, for example, claims that the [congregational] culture "consists of physical artifacts, patterns of activities, and the language and story that embellish those objects with meaning."[7] In other words, the culture of congregation is comprised of, first and foremost, *why* people congregate to form a faith community and *what* they come together to *do*. Emphasizing the importance of practicing rather than merely believing, social historians and cultural anthropologists also have paid attention to "lived religion" and its ever-changing dynamics: "The patterns that make up lived religion in any time and place reveal how ordinary men and women make their way through a set of choices, fashioning, as they do so, a mode of being religious that is responsible to needs that arise within social life."[8] Indeed, as Alasdair MacIntyre argues, "practices always have histories and [that] at any given moment what a practice is depends on a mode of understanding it which has been transmitted often through many generations."[9] Centering on the embodied, practiced, transmitted, and lived religion of Korean American Christians, the first part of this Korean American companion guide attempts to provide a social history of their faith communities. For contemporary practices of Korean American Christianity reflect not only the history of religious ideas but also the history of the formation of religious organizations and human actions. Consequently, this chapter emphasizes the centrality of Korean American agency for incorporating survival strategies and negotiating identities for both individuals and a racial-ethnic group through Korean American practices of Christianity.

Documenting a social history of Korean American Protestant faith communities in the United States is more than an assemblage of dates, acts, and names, as Asian Americanist Gary Y. Okihiro has asserted. Pointing to a new way of documenting a history called "family album history," Okihiro contends that "a family album history is inspired by the strands in Asian American history that reach to those regularly absent from the gallery of 'great men,' to activities excluded from the inventory of 'significant events,' and to regions usually ignored by the worlds of science."[10] As such, it overcomes limitations imposed by deeply masculine accounts of historical recordings, communal histories written by outsiders, and forgotten and omitted stories of the dispossessed. Just as individual family albums may "help to define a personal identity and locate its place within the social order and to connect that person to others, from one generation to the next, like the exchanging snapshots around family and friends,"[11] ethnic family albums can help to probe the intricate relationship between individuals and their community and to uncover emerging themes and paradigms of their lived experience.[12] Employing the "family album history" as both a methodology and a construct is not only instrumental for writing a social history of Korean American Protestant faith communities; it is also advantageous in another way: it fills the gap in census data and in other quantitative studies. For unlike national census forms used in other European and Latin American countries, "the U.S. Census never asked citizens to report their personal religious affiliations,"[13] and "Korean" as a racial-ethnic category in the U.S. Census did not appear until the year 1970.

What follows, then, are discussions organized around four historical periods of the Korean American church in the United States: 1) 1903–1950; 2) 1950–1968; 3) 1968–1988/1992; and 4) 1988/1992–present. Each historical period is segmented according to how Korean Americans formed and experienced Christianity, on the one hand, and how they responded to the broader sociopolitical structures of their times in the United States, on the other hand. For each historical segment, an overview of demographic characteristics of Korean Americans, the meaning and experiences of faith communities, and, when applied, selected stories of lived experiences are offered. For "narrative matters,"[14] and these stories can provide deeper understanding of the agency of Korean Americans in negotiating their own racial-ethnic identities, religion, economic opportunities, and gender (re-) construction in the United States.

THE EXILE COMMUNITY: 1903–1950

Discussions on the discovery of gold in California and about labor shortages on Hawaiian plantations and work crews for the building of the transcontinental railroads in the middle of the nineteenth century provide an irreplaceable ecopolitical context for documenting Chinese American history in the United States.[15] Similarly, discussions on the role of Christian missionaries spreading a peculiar "gospel" of the United States as "heaven on earth" and the "land flowing with milk and honey" in order to offset the ethnic labor politics on Hawaiian plantations at the dawn of the Japanese annexation of the Korean peninsula became the oft-cited ecoreligious context for understanding Korean immigration to the United States. Along with the civil unrest caused by famine, poverty, and constant attacks and influences by foreign powers—the push factors—Christian missionaries from the United States seized the opportunity to recruit new Korean converts for both spiritual and economic causes—the pull factors. Take for example, Horace Newton Allen,[16] the first Protestant missionary from the United States, who went to Korea in September 1884.[17] As a Christian missionary, he provided an important "pulpit service" for officially arranging

Korean labor immigration with Hawaiian plantation owners[18] to break the labor unrest and to force down wages of their predominantly Japanese work force.[19] Horace G. Underwood, the Presbyterian missionary who went to Korea in April 1885, and Henry G. Appenzeller, the first United Methodist missionary who arrived a month later,[20] also actively cooperated with the U.S. Ministry of Labor to recruit Korean laborers for Hawaiian plantation owners. Thus the early eclipse of Korean immigration points to not only transnational politics among Korea, Japan, and the United States but also to the interplay of economic and religious undercurrents. A closer examination of the "pulpit service" offered by Christian missionaries during late nineteenth-century Korea provides a critical lens with which to view the history of Korean American experiences of Christianity in the United States. Immigration policies that affected Korean Americans not only shaped their migration and resettlement patterns but also reconfigured religious experiences.

Although there are a few records of Koreans traveling to the United States as early as 1888,[21] the entrance of Koreans as labor immigrants to the United States started in 1903.[22] On January 13, 1903, one hundred and one Koreans—composed of fifty-five men, twenty-one women, and twenty-five children—entered Honolulu, Hawaii.[23] During the first three years from 1903 to 1905, a total of 7,226 Koreans came to work on Hawaiian sugar plantations. Among them, approximately 6,000 were adult males whose ages ranged from their early twenties to their late thirties, and some 1,000 women, with several hundred children. Some scholars have pointed to this pattern of Korean "family" labor unit as a distinct characteristic that sets them apart from virtually all male laborers from China and, to a lesser degree, from Japan.[24] Clearly the sex ratio of the first wave of Korean immigrants was far from being balanced; but compared to the highly skewed sex ratio among Chinese and Japanese laborers at the time, experiences of the "mutilated family"[25] were not as widely spread among Korean male laborers. Further, there are at least two other distinct demographic characteristics of these first 7,226 Koreans that resist attempts to homogenize them as unskilled proletariat from Korea.

First, although they were all treated as unskilled and semi-skilled laborers by Hawaiian plantation owners at the time of their arrival, only about 60 percent remained in Hawaii by 1905 and about 50 percent by the time Japan officially annexed Korea in 1910. Some 1,000 returned to Korea; another 2,000 moved onto the mainland (mostly to California); and 1,033 were reported as immigrating to Mexico in 1905.[26] This trend of "moving on" among the first wave of Korean immigrants can be explained from several vantage points, but their diverse social-class backgrounds prior to entering the United States also provide an important clue. They were semi-skilled urbanites, low-ranking government officials, peasants, ex-soldiers, students, and political refugees from Korea.[27] Other records also illustrate that they were originally from Inchon, Busan, Wonsan, Chinnampo, and Seoul,[28] all fairly large "metro" cities and port cities. These metro and port cities were also known as important religious sites where massive and zealous Christian conversions were taking place in Korea. For example, it is now well documented that some 40 percent of the first 101 Koreans who came to the United States in 1903 were from the same Christian church in Inchon, the Youngdong Church of Rev. George Herbert Jones.[29] Furthermore, Korean and Korean American scholars estimate that approximately 40 to 60 percent of all Koreans who came to the United States before 1905 were converted Christians.[30]

Indeed, the ticket to voyage across the Pacific Ocean for Koreans came with the price tag of attaining a (new) religious identity. This religious affiliation of Korean labor immigrants is another characteristic that distinguishes them from the earlier Chinese and Japanese laborers. Within the first several months of resettling in the "Christian" United States, Korean laborers formed the Hawaii Methodist Church in November of 1903 and the Hawaii Korean Anglican Church in February of 1905. Among the first Koreans who ventured onto the mainland, they established the San Francisco Korean Methodist Church in September 1903 and the Los Angeles Presbyterian Church in September 1905.[31] All four first Korean churches were formed prior to the termination of Korean immigration by the Japanese government in 1905 and have become the first Korean American faith communities in the United States.

From 1910 to the passing of the Immigration Act in 1924, which prohibited entrance of Asian immigrants, a total of 1,066 picture brides[32] came into the United States. In addition, some 900 students, intellectuals, and political refugees who had been involved in the anti-Japanese movement in Korea also came. Since no official Korean immigration took place from 1924 to 1950, no data is shown in records of the U.S. Immigration and Naturalization Services during this historical time period. The experience of exclusion and isolation of Korean Americans was further reiterated by the fact that no Korean-born person could become a naturalized U.S. citizen until the passage of the McCarran Walter Act in 1952.

Legal constraints to bar Korean Americans from becoming U.S. citizens would further ignite Korean Americans' nationalism to participate actively in the movement for Korean independence from Japan. Indeed, most of the surviving records from this period testify to unusually frequent gatherings at the church and active participation of "churched" Korean Americans in the Korea Independence Movement. The importance of the Christian church as a physical site for Korean Americans to gather to "donate significant portions of their wages to support the provisional government"[33] and as a religious cause for its adherents to sign and send numerous petitions to U.S. President Theodore Roosevelt advocating the national independence of Korea cannot be overexaggerated.

As a racial ethnic institution, the Korean American church also hosted and trained its own political leaders for the cause of Korean independence. Among many Korean American Christian politicians, perhaps the story of Syngman

Rhee can depict a peculiar experience of religion and community in Korean America at the time. Syngman Rhee, who became the first president of the Republic of Korea (South Korea) after Korean independence from Japan, was a labor immigrant who arrived in the United States in 1905. After studying at Harvard and Princeton, Rhee formed the Han-in Tong-nip Kyo-whe (Korean Independence Church) in Hawaii and pastored churched Korean Americans during the 1920s. Korean independence from Japan was achieved in 1945, and with the landing of the U.S. troops in Southern Korea and the Soviet Union troops in Northern Korea, he returned to Korea from the United States in 1946. As a result of the U.N.-supported separate elections in South and North Korea, Syngman Rhee became the first president of South Korea. Throughout his thirty-some years of political life in both the United States and Korea, the Korean Independence Church in Hawaii provided "a base for his political activities."[34] This is not to say that virtually all Korean Americans living in the U.S. had converted to Christianity by 1950, but it is true that they had become extensively and predominantly a "churched" population. Whether Korean Americans attended the church predominantly for political cause or for religious reasons, their experiences of Christian religion do not point to a mutually exclusive dichotomy between politics and religion. Clearly, Korean American experiences of their own church points to a complementary continuum between the political and the religious, and a cultural continuum between Koreans abroad and on the Korean peninsula. As a people in exile whose experiences are marked by double colonialism, Korean Americans have formed and founded their faith community in the United States in their own racial ethnic churches. By 1950, there were "32 [Christian] congregations serving 2,800 Koreans" in Hawaii alone and "a similar number of Christian churches on the mainland."[35] These churches became the main community centers to address multifaceted survival needs of their adherents, and they provided programs and services such as translation and interpretation, job placement, counseling, legal aids, conflict resolution strategies, and language classes.

THE HYBRID COMMUNITY: 1950–1968

While strengthening ethnic bonds may be the main characteristic of the exile people, the faith communities of the "second wave" of Korean immigrants who entered the United States after 1950 resemble a combination of exile and immigrant models. Defining main differences between exiles and immigrants rests largely on two concepts and experiences: dislocation and home base. Exile is defined as "the condition of voluntary and involuntary separating from one's place of birth" and is often offset by "continuous bonds to the lost homeland,"[36] whereas immigrants are people who made conscious decisions to leave the birth land in order to reestablish a new home. Since most of the second wave of

Korean immigrants came to the United States as three distinct groups—(war) orphans, wives of U.S. servicemen, and students—their experiences of dislocation and home base vary along the continuum of voluntary and involuntary leaving of the birthplace and of intentionally or unintentionally naming the U.S. as their own home base. Hence, the second wave of immigrants from Korea point to another set of diverse and hybrid characteristics of Korean American communities in the United States.

From 1955 to 1966, 6,293 Korean orphans were adopted in the United States, mostly through the Holt Adoption agency.[37] Their racial compositions were 46 percent "white Koreans," 13 percent "black Koreans," and the rest (41 percent) "full Koreans."[38] Although the adoption of Korean children continues today, a majority of 6,293 war orphans are "Amerasians" and what Velina H. Houston calls the "Asian hybrid"[39] produced by the Korean war. Besides a few nationwide studies of adopted Korean orphans by D. Kim in 1972, D. Kim and S. P. Kim in 1977, and Hurh and Kim in 1984, few, if any, systematic studies and information are available. Some religious and humanitarian attempts to address issues and problems of Korean adoptees in the United States have been initiated recently. The Korean Community Presbyterian Church of Atlanta (PC(USA)), for example, has launched its annual "Festival for Adopted Families" since 1996. And by 1999, the church's annual ministry for Korean adoptees and their families had grown to a gathering of 280 family members. The church hopes "to turn the event into a true festival with booths that offer everything from ethnic food to cultural information and resources to help parents understand their children."[40] Integrating stories and experiences of Korean adoptees as another important chapter in the history of Korean America, however, is one that is yet to be written.

Under the terms of the 1952 McCarran Walter Act,[41] another under-studied and silenced category of Koreans started to enter the United States: Korean wives of American G.I.s. From 1951 to 1964, 6,423 Korean women came to the United States as "war brides" or "G.I. wives." Mainly due to the U.S. military presence in South Korea, this influx of Korean immigrant wives of U.S. servicemen continues today. For example, the average number of Korean wives of U.S. servicemen coming into the United States was some 1,500 a year during the 1960s and about 2,300 in the 1970s.[42] A few scholars have documented demographic characteristics and marital adjustment of Korean wives of G.I.s.[43] Living in strategically isolated locations near military bases and being stigmatized and segregated from their co-ethnics for out-marrying, experiences of Korean wives of U.S. servicemen are rendered secondary in both Korean American communities and the United States at large. While many of these Korean wives of U.S. servicemen sponsored bringing in their relatives from Korea under the Immigration Act of 1965, they have yet to be credited as the very backbone of contemporary Korean America.

In addition to these two hybrid and silenced groups of Korean Americans, an estimated 5,000 students also came to the United States between 1950 and 1965.

Very little has been documented about this group of people for yet another reason. A majority of these students eventually and inevitably became un- or underdocumented U.S. aliens. Since the student visa stipulates that the duration of legal stay is to be determined by the attainment of academic credentials or other reasons for terminating study, most Koreans who overstayed "naturally" became illegal aliens. Remembering that the very pillar of the Korean American community leaders were once "illegal U.S. aliens" is perhaps unsettling. Even more unsettling, however, it that these Korean Americans' use of religion, and especially Christianity, was their very survival mechanism.

Caution against an overemphasis on the important functions U.S. missionaries played in Korea and in Korean American lives is well intended, because the history and content of Korean American Protestant faith communities attest to the agency of Korean Americans. When assessing the access to socioeconomic resources, however, the religious identity of Korean Americans and their ties to U.S. missionaries demonstrate a clear and strong correlation to their survival and economic success. For example, Kyung Won Lee, who came to the United States in 1950 and became "a pioneer Korean American journalist in English,"[44] testifies to the missionary zeal to offer scholarships to Koreans who would study Christian theology at U.S. colleges and universities. Reflecting his own status as "one of the original FOBs" (fresh-off-the-boats) in 1950, K. Lee claims that most Korean immigrants during the 1950s were Christians: "We were targets of Christian embrace."[45] He adds that "Koreans who had some connection with a church could get a scholarship, but I never had any connection with the church, so I came on my own. The others had scholarships."[46] Since U.S. missionaries actively recruited Koreans to study Christian theology and to spread Christianity, they offered scholarships to those who would become Christians and study theology. At the time of the political and economic upheaval in the divided Korea, many (male) Koreans made decisions to put their souls in the hands of U.S. missionaries as an exchange for a ticket to the "land flowing with milk and honey." Hence, professing the correct religious identity and having contact with U.S. missionaries were two direct causal factors for Korean American survival. Given these historical memories of infusing a religious identity with educational opportunities in the United States, it is no surprise to find that so many Korean Americans aggregate in their own faith communities in search for survival, resources, and spiritual solace.

THE IMMIGRANT COMMUNITY: 1968–1988/1992

Lumping all Korean Americans living in the U.S. as a monolithic category called the "post-1965 immigrants" calls for a critical reexamination of the history and politics of immigration policies.[47] Too often literature focuses on reframing Korean (and Asian) Americans as all new and post-1965 immigrants and their religions as various attempts to transplant ethnic traditions in the United States; it also points to the tenacious process of myth making based on the assumed "teleology of Americanization."[48] The teleology of Americanization entails conceptualizing immigrants, their cultures, and "racial-ethnic differences largely as a matter of something 'left behind.'"[49] This insistence on "a time before U.S. entry and on cultures separate from U.S. Anglo-identity" is also called the "immigration logos."[50] Contrary to the "teleology of Americanization" and the "immigration logos," however, ethnicity is never fixed but something that is always being made anew, just as in the politics of individual identity formation.

Systemic and detailed information on Korean Americans has become available since 1970 because it was the first year the term "Korean" as a distinct ethnic name was used in the U.S. Census instead of the previously used "other Asian" category. The U.S. Census counted 70,598 Koreans by 1970; 357,393 by 1980; 798,849 by 1990;[51] and 1.07 million by 2000.[52] Clearly, these census accounts demonstrate a drastic increase in the Korean American population; within the first decade from 1970 to 1980, the Korean American population increased almost 400 percent, and during the second decade from 1980 to 1990, another 100 percent. A closer look at demographic characteristics of the Korean American population also points to two distinctive SES (socioeconomic status) groupings of the post-1965 Korean immigrants. While Koreans who came into the United States under the 1965 Immigration Act are mostly well-educated, middle-class professionals, Koreans who arrived under the Immigration and Nationality Act Amendment of 1976—which limited the number of entries for professionals by favoring family reunification of the U.S. citizens—come from a variety of educational and occupational backgrounds.

Given these demographic differences between two groups—the pre-1976 (and the post-1965) and the post-1976 Korean immigrants—what Edna Bonacich refers to as the difference of class "background" is insightful: although the concept of class or SES came to mean class "background" in contemporary America, there is a clear difference between "the class from which one has come" and "the class into which one is moving."[53] That is to say, regardless of various class backgrounds, most Korean Americans tend to consider their present SES as a temporary, and therefore transitional, stage to achieve their own American dream in the land of opportunity. This robust striving to achieve the American dream, in effect, enabled Korean Americans to form and experience faith communities across class lines. This is not to depict Korean American faith communities as truly inclusive and egalitarian religious institutions, but to emphasize the significance of the "striving class" (and not so much of class "background") in the Korean American mind-set.[54]

The significance of the concept of "striving class" among Korean Americans and their experiences of faith communities across class lines are subtexted by at least two closely intertwined macro and micro dynamics. First, Korean (and other Asian) Americans are "racialized" and therefore locked out of the broad

U.S. labor market.[55] Since they were originally recruited as cheap labor forces and often isolated and suppressed as a racial ethnic "minority," they "could not be a part of the working class and certainly could not develop strong American class consciousness."[56] This economic isolation, in turn, contributed to "the distortion of capital formation within [Korean] American communities."[57] Second, even as Korean Americans are rendered another racial ethnic minority, most of the post-1965, first-generation immigrants' simplistic understanding of race precludes them from critical assessment on their own American dream. Their crude perception of race follows something like this: "We are Asians! We look different! Therefore, we are being discriminated against! The remedy is to work harder and to show the Whites that we are just as good if not better."[58] Indeed, they do work harder. An exceptionally high number of Korean Americans are self-employed and their length of daily labor is often stretched from 10 to 12 hours.[59] This unusually high level of self-employment and lengthy labor hours testify to the structural disadvantages Korean Americans experience on the labor market.

With this type of simple racial analysis and the undying effort to achieve upward mobility, Korean Americans experienced rapid population growth and exponential church growth from 1968 to 1988/1992. Reflecting the very ethos of the Korean American belief of the American dream during this time period, their faith communities also enthusiastically embraced a peculiar gospel of equating Korean Americans as "God's chosen people." It is thus no surprise that a prominent Korean American theologian's articulation of Korean immigrants as a faithful people obediently responding to God's call to pilgrimage God's promised land—America[60]—swept Korean American faith communities during the same period. Korean Americans have not only become synonymous with a "churched population" but also self-selected survivors as the "chosen people" en route to religious pilgrimage in the United States. Korean American success is now God's will, and every obedient subject of God will do his or her best to bring about God's will on earth.

Another often-neglected aspect of understanding Korean American faith communities during this time period is the feminization of faith communities. Korean women, both in Korea and in the United States, are more likely than Korean men to be affiliated with and actively participate in the church.[61] Along with this gendered religious affiliation, economically based immigration laws are also an important causal factor for feminizing faith communities. The stated dual purpose of the 1965 Immigration Act[62] is "to facilitate family reunification and to admit skilled workers needed by the U.S. economy."[63] By 1975, however, women constituted a numerical majority of immigrants from South Korea and from other Asian countries, such as China, Taiwan, the Philippines, and Japan.[64] The most oft-cited reasons for the proportionally higher number of women immigrants from South Korea include the continuous influx of Korean wives of U.S. servicemen entering as non-quota immigrants, importation of nurses and other medical technicians who also happen to be mostly women, and more recently, the growth of female-intensive industries[65] in the United States.[66] While being subject to the "female ghettoes of employment,"[67] Korean American women tend to perceive and experience their participation in the paid labor market as "an extension of their family obligations"[68] as daughters, wives, and mothers in order to contribute to family survival and well-being. And as they actively participate in both paid and unpaid labor markets, they also make up 60 to 65 percent of their faith communities. Within their own faith communities, Korean American women often find that their contributions and experiences have been rendered secondary.[69]

THE HYPHENATED AND TRANSNATIONAL COMMUNITY: 1988/1992 TO PRESENT

The year 1988 was the first year when the "return immigration"[70] of Korean American families to South Korea took place in a significant number; and the year 1992 brought about profound leadership changes in Korean American communities. The significant influx of reverse migrants and the sudden and sweeping leadership change in any community begs for explanation, and Korean American communities are no exception. What follows then is a brief discussion of the two historical events in 1988 and 1992 that influenced the making of the new Korean American consciousness. To classify the years 1988/1992 as a watershed period marking the Korean American community as transnational and hyphenated is to recognize the significance of both micro and macro changes in the formation of the Korean American consciousness.

Seoul, the capital of South Korea, hosted the World Olympic Games in 1988. The glaring display of economic boom and industrial progress depicted on television screens caused both pride and a keen sense of dislocation in the Korean American consciousness. The remembered "homeland" many had left behind was plagued by political repression and economic struggle and was in need of swift and fundamental social reformation, if not revolution. The South Korea portrayed on television screens during the Olympic Games, however, was full of happy and proud smiles of Koreans who seemed untouched by poisonous racism. While Korean Americans struggled to turn their life journeys into "success stories" by putting in extra hours of hard labor to actualize the American dream, it was as though the entire country of South Korea had made itself a huge success story—an "economic miracle"—by becoming a member of the "five little dragons" (or "tigers") of the global economy.[71] Experiencing cognitive dissonance, some Korean Americans started to pack their belongings to make the trip back across the Pacific Ocean in significant numbers beginning in 1988. *The Korean Journal* and *The Southeast News* reported that some 3,000 Korean Americans reverse-immigrated to South Korea from the United States in 1988 and another 4,000 Korean Americans in 1989.[72] Parenthetically, data released by the U.S. Immigration and Naturalization Service also illustrates the steady decline in the number of Korean immigrants to the United States from 1988 to 1991 and the more drastic decline from 1992 to 1995.[73]

Several years after the 1988 Olympic Games in Seoul, much of the South Central spread of Korea-town in Los Angeles was broken into, looted, and burned to the ground from April 29 to May 2, 1992. As of May 6, 1992, the estimated damage of property and business loss of Korean-owned business in L.A. amounted to $346,962,394.[74] Thousands of Korean Americans lost their means of livelihood and the ability to even dream the American dream. The shock and the rage against the Rodney King verdict and the aftermath of the L.A. "riot"/"uprising" was not contained within the city of L.A. alone but spread throughout the United States. News alert and finger-pointing against "different" racial and class boundaries went on for some time as people attempted to make sense of what had happened to their own communities. The whereabouts of the National Guard and the Los Angeles Police Department during the riot/ uprising was investigated; African American residents blamed rude Korean American store owners; Korean Americans pointed out Hispanic American looters; and Hispanic Americans criticized African American violence. Headlines in Korean newspapers, such as "Korean Americans as Sacrificial Lambs" and "The American Dream Gone to Ashes"[75] point to the utter despair, rage, and injustice experienced by Korean Americans during the riot/uprising. In fact, the impact of the L.A. riot/uprising brought about such a fundamental change in the Korean American consciousness that Korean Americans call the incident the "*Sa-I-Ku*."[76] The literal meaning of "*Sa-I-Ku*" is "4–2–9" in Korean, which signifies the date April 29. Indeed, the "*Sa-I-Ku*" and its aftermath has led Korean Americans to reassess their own socioeconomic and political locations in the United States. And their urgent need to give voices to the shared experiences prompted rather rapidly both explicit and implicit shifts in the landscape of Korean American community leadership. Korean Americans who are fluent in English rose above to give voices to experiences of the "*Sa-I-Ku*" from Korean American perspectives. To name the loss and rage and to demand at least financial compensation, the Korean-speaking community leaders who enjoyed virtually sole access to the leadership positions found themselves relying on the English-speaking (often called second-generation) Korean Americans.

This leadership change, from the predominantly Korean-speaking first generation to the mostly English-speaking Korean Americans in the community, was not necessarily a "natural" generational shift in leadership as in other racial ethnic communities; it was mostly a result of a particular historical event that necessitated such a drastic change. Since the influx of Korean immigrants coming to the United States has been continuous since 1968, the Korean American (faith) community leadership tends to be handed down and replaced by new first-generation immigrants from Korea rather than by the second generation. Rather than community leadership being transmitted from the first generation to the second, and then to the subsequent generation, the predominantly English-speaking second- and subsequent-generation Korean Americans tend to form new faith (and other social) communities of their own, often set apart from their first-generation-oriented organizations. And these English-speaking faith communities of Korean Americans are increasingly becoming pan-Asian rather than insisting on ethnically specified, hyphenated Korean as a salient organizational identity. Given that 72.7 percent of Korean Americans are born outside of the United States[77] and 51.6 percent of Korean Americans "do not speak English very well,"[78] the emerging trend of the English-speaking Korean Americans representing Korean American communities at large also demands a close look and further probing. Of particular interest here, however, is that a combination of the turbulent economic uprootednesss of the "*Sa-I-Ku*" and the cognitive dissonance from the 1988 Olympic Games in Seoul resulted in the fundamental change: carving out a political space that enabled the predominantly English-speaking Korean American generation(s) to gain both voice and visibility in the context of Korean America and the mainstream United States, on the one hand, and a blurring of the traditionally drawn boundary between Koreans and Korean Americans via fluid and migratory movement transnationally, on the other hand. The surge of the English-speaking "generation," then, needs to be examined as a necessary survival strategy of Korean Americans living in the post-1992 United States rather than merely as a "natural" phenomenon.

Terms such as "generation" and "generation gap" are often used to describe and explain a wide range of differences in Korean America. Although the "new" generation of Korean Americans are not only second-generation but also 1.5, third- and subsequent-generation, and mixed-race Korean Americans, the fixation of the predominantly English-speaking Korean Americans as the "second generation" seems to take place. Given this particular usage of the term, can "generation" be operationalized as a useful concept and a measurement to understand complex experiences of religion in Korean America or lend itself to more debate and confusion? A number of studies have focused on the religious experiences of the English-speaking Korean Americans. David Kim's and Antony W. Alumkal's studies, for example, stress the religious rather than ethnic identity as the core identity shared among the second-generation Korean American Christians.[79] Helen Lee's and Minho Song's studies document the "quiet exodus" phenomenon of the English-speaking Korean Americans from their Korean-speaking parents' church.[80] Put together, while the thesis of the ethnic salience for forming a religious community is no longer relevant to understand the second-generation Korean American Christians, other studies allude to a combination of more complex both/and and neither/nor. For example, Kelly Chong's study based in the Chicago area and Karen Chai's ethnographic study of the English-speaking

Korean American church in the Boston area[81] both highlight the complex process and rationales among church members for attending a pan-Asian rather than a Korean American church. Although all these studies on the second and subsequent generation's experiences of religion are based in the particular region and use different methodologies and approaches, they point to this apparent trend: while forming a faith community based on the shared ethnic identity is no longer relevant for the English-speaking generation, their race identity in the United States plays an instrumental role for forming pan-Asian faith communities.

Why does occasional focus on generations and a generation gap emerge at some periods of history, and not others? Why is the historical period from 1988/1992 to present conceptualized as mainly a time of generational conflict? Here, Mannheim's understanding of generation is helpful. Unlike other scholars who defined "generation" as more or less an age/birth cohort, Mannheim emphasized the importance of sharing the same social change and events as a group to the formation of "generational uniqueness."[82] For him, generation is not determined so much by sharing the same demographic characteristics such as birth cohort or age group, but by sharing the group consciousness that resulted from experiencing common historical events of significance. In this sense, Korean Americans who experienced the keen sense of cognitive dissonance during the 1988 Olympic Games in Seoul and/or the "generational uniqueness" via the "Sa-I-Ku" mark a new generation of Korean Americans. This preference of defining "generation" as a matter of attaining and sharing group consciousness is also consistent with the increasingly blurred boundaries among nation-states in the late twentieth century. As Elaine Kim has noted, "Yesterday's young Korean American immigrants have labored beside their immigrant farm-worker parents in segregated rural California. . . . Today's young Korean Americans probably watched *The Wonderful World of Disney* on television in Seoul as a child and today rent Korean-language videos at a Los Angeles mini-mall store."[83] Whether English-speaking Korean American Christians turn to their pan-Asian or reethnicized Korean American churches, they seem to hold fast to selective memories and rituals that make them "Korean American" in the United States.

As Goellnicht asserts, all historical analysis is always "partial, incomplete, and provisional."[84] In a way, history is "nothing other than the reconstruction and redistribution of a pretended order of things, the interpretation or even transformation of documents given and frozen into monuments."[85] What has been attempted in this chapter is thus a provisional social history of Korean American Christians that makes their religious experiences and organizations the center of such a reconstruction. The sweeping scope and formation of Korean American faith communities that this chapter attempts to chronicle provide a picture of dynamic change in community and in the agency of people that is anything but simple. Recognizing the never-ending nature of a provisional work, the next section of this Korean American companion guide offers an in-depth look at eight main practices of lived religion in the Korean American church. Together with this brief social history of Korean American churches, the next section will provide new insights for understanding how Korean American Christians practice, gather, and live out their lives by remembering and reshaping their own sense of people-hood in multicultural America.

Chapter 2

This Is the Day

The Practice of Keeping the Sabbath

Her day starts at five in the morning. While still dark out, she gets out of bed, throws on some clothes, quickly washes up (the minimal, of course, no time for makeup), and tiptoes out the front door so as not to awaken the whole family from deep sleep. She drives half an hour to pick up a high school student in her youth group. They have the system down to a tee. When she arrives at his house, she gives a signal with her headlights. He sees the blinking lights and sneaks out of the house. In his hands are two cups: one, a cup of milk; another, a cup of coffee. He gets in the car and gives her the cup of milk to drink first and then the cup of coffee for the journey. They drive for another ten minutes to the church for the dawn prayer meeting (sae-byuk ki-do-whe),[1] which starts at 6 a.m. Everyone there is somewhat subdued, without the usual energy of greeting and chatting with each other. Tired bodies, minds preoccupied with prayer concerns . . . the prayer meeting lasts about half an hour. Hymns are sung, Scripture is read, and a brief homily follows. Then some time is given for everyone to pray. After the prayer meeting, she takes the teenager home on the way to her own house. She goes home and gets ready for the day's work.

—from Su Yon's recollection
of her daily practice of
dawn prayer meeting

Dawn prayer meeting is one of many practices in which Korean American Christians participate to keep sacred time and sacred space.[2] This practice of worshiping and praying together serves as a temporal and spatial center that enables Korean American Christians to gather as a community to revitalize

17

their lives and to realign their relationships with God, with each other, and with their family members. Understanding Korean American Christian practices in terms of *time* and *space* is crucial to understanding Korean American Christian spirituality.

THE SPIRITUAL GEOGRAPHY OF SACRED SPACE

> How lovely is your dwelling place,
>   O LORD of hosts!
> My soul longs, indeed it faints
>   for the courts of the LORD;
> my heart and my flesh sing for joy
>   to the living God.
>
> Even the sparrow finds a home,
>   and the swallow a nest for herself,
>   where she may lay her young,
> at your altars, O LORD of hosts,
>   my King and my God.
> Happy are those who live in your house,
>   ever singing your praise.
>   . . .
> For a day in your courts is better
>   than a thousand elsewhere.
> I would rather be a doorkeeper in the house of my God
>   than live in the tents of wickedness.
>   (Ps. 84:1–4, 10)

In thinking about keeping Sabbath, we think first about setting *time* aside. In fact, it is true to say that traditional Western metaphysics is preoccupied with "time." Words and concepts like "eternity," "forever," and "life everlasting" are measured in time. Korean American practices, however, are spatial as well as temporal. While individual daily devotion and Bible study have an important place in the faith practice of Korean American Christians, the gathering as a body of believers in a designated place holds a special significance. Furthermore, the "land," and, more specifically, the "new land," has an important meaning for a people who experienced colonization and displacement in their own land and who im/migrated to new lands. Therefore, as the psalmist sings, the place of worship or prayer is an important factor in the whole experience of practicing faith. It becomes the spiritual geography of a community of faith. In particular, the mountain and the sanctuary are the two prominent spaces that Korean American Christians deem sacred.

Koreans have long believed that spiritual energy is intense in the mountains. Therefore, people of faith regularly go up the mountain to pray, regardless of their faith tradition. A Korean American pastor ministering to an English-speaking congregation in Chicago has incorporated this practice into his Christian education program. After a three-month-long Bible study series, he takes the congregation up to the "prayer mountain," a mountain he has designated as a sacred place to wrestle with God.

Another important sacred space is the sanctuary, and within the sanctuary, the altar. An important image that grounds the spirituality of Korean American Christians is the image of Jacob at Bethel. In Genesis, Jacob builds an altar after he awakes from a dream where he sees angels ascending and descending and senses the presence of God. He takes the stone he had used for his pillow and sets it up for a pillar and pours oil on it. At this altar, he bargains with God:

> "If God will be with me, and will keep me in this way that I go, and will give me bread to eat and clothing to wear, so that I come again to my father's house in peace, then the LORD shall be my God, and this stone, which I have set up for a pillar, shall be God's house; and of all that you give me I will surely give one-tenth to you." (Gen. 28:20–22)

Jacob builds an altar in recognition of God's presence, and he makes a vow. For Korean American Christians, this practice of building a physical space to mark God's presence is important; keeping and tending the altar is considered another important task of the faithful.

This important task of keeping and tending the altar plays itself out in the way Korean Americans keep Sabbath. Explicitly and implicitly, one is expected to worship every Sunday in one's own church in one's own sanctuary. They talk about "keeping the altar" (*jae-dan-eul ji-kin-da*), where by physically worshiping in their own church, they are watching over and keeping the altar. So in keeping the Sabbath, it is important to keep the altar. Recognizing a certain space as sacred draws some pastors to take off their shoes when preaching in the pulpit, as Moses did in the presence of God.

Therefore, to make one's faith practice right, the place where one chooses to engage in a particular practice of faith becomes important. One of the authors shares the following story told by her pastor to emphasize this important connection between keeping the sacred space and practicing the dawn prayer:

> A man decides that he will get up early in the morning to go up the mountain to pray. The first morning, he gets up and goes up to the top of the mountain and prays. On his way back down to his house, he says to himself, "Why should God only be on the top of the mountain? God must be in the middle of the mountain." So the next morning he gets up and goes halfway up the mountain and prays. On his way back down to his house, he says to himself, "Why should God only be in the middle of the mountain? God must also be at the foot of the mountain." The next morning, he gets up and goes to the foot of the mountain and prays. On his way back to the house, he says to himself, "Why should God only be at the foot of the mountain? God must also be in my bed." The next morning he wakes up to pray in his bed, but cannot keep his eyes open. So he falls asleep.

Throughout the story, the pastor would emphasize the importance of getting up early and making the effort to gather together at a sacred space and at a sacred time.

THE SPIRITUAL RHYTHM OF SACRED TIME

My heart is steadfast, O God, my heart is steadfast;
   I will sing and make melody.
   Awake, my soul!
Awake, O harp and lyre!
   I will awake the dawn.
(Ps. 108:1–2)

Dawn prayer meeting is a common practice of Korean American Christians. It is a way for Korean Americans to set aside time and space to gather at the beginning of the day. The format usually consists of hymn singing, Scripture reading, a short sermon or reflection, followed by a long period of prayer, both collective and individual. It is a mini-service with an emphasis on prayer, a practice adapted from that of Buddhist monks, who hold an early morning devotion every day at four o'clock. This practice was Christianized and zealously followed. In fact, it is said that at one point, in order to be spiritually zealous, the Christians began to hold their prayer meetings even earlier than the Buddhists.[3]

Similar to Jacob's bargaining at the altar at Bethel, the dawn prayer meetings serve as one of the most important channels to demand divine intervention in the lives of Korean American Christians. One can say that the practice of dawn prayer meeting measures the spiritual temperature of both the individuals and the church. For instance, if the pastor or church leaders feel that the church is not growing or is spiritually weak, they will begin holding dawn prayer meetings, even if it is not their regular practice, and they will invite all the congregants to participate. In their minds, it is not enough that the leaders pray on behalf of the church; everyone must make a concerted effort to pray together for church growth. Other reasons for attending the dawn prayer meetings are to work out certain problems, to discern the will of God, or just to talk honestly and openly with God about their painful immigrant lives.

Rising at an "ungodly" hour may seem to dishonor the body, particularly since many Korean immigrants work long hours. Moreover, for those whose body clock starts later in the morning, the demands of this practice can be unnatural to their own body rhythms. A Korean American woman talks about what this Korean overemphasis on rising early taught her as a child, implicitly and explicitly. To illustrate her point, she jokes about how she was oppressed by the children's song that says, "Children of a new nation arise early; in our great nation, there are no lazy people." The song equates rising early with industriousness, without giving any consideration to differences in biorhythms. Thus, early risers are deemed industrious, while late risers are considered lazy.

Any kind of dominant expectation that does not take individual differences into consideration can be oppressive, and, in this case, harmful to the body. However, this practice can also be viewed as a way of honoring the body. Koreans believe that *ki (ch'i* in Chinese), the power of life or vitality,[4] is strong at dawn. Some might argue that to get up when *ki* is strong and align oneself with God is to honor the body regardless of the biorhythm. One prominent practice in Korea that is based on this understanding is early morning hiking in the mountains. Many women and men, particularly the elderly, hike up the mountain, usually to the site of a nice, clear spring. The water that springs from the depth of the mountain is supposed to be filled with the pure spirit of the mountain that fortifies the human spirit. Such water is called "living water" (*sang-soo*). The hikers drink it to their satisfaction before coming down the mountain.

The Sacred Day: The Lord's Day

> Remember the sabbath day, and keep it holy. Six days you shall labor and do all your work. But the seventh day is a sabbath to the LORD your God; you shall not do any work—you, your son or your daughter, your male or female slave, your livestock, or the alien resident in your towns. (Exod. 20:8–10)

Sabbath keeping, by setting aside time to come together to worship on the Lord's Day, is possibly the most well practiced of all of the Ten Commandments. This commandment is so zealously followed that Korean Christians have replaced the word "Sunday" (*il-yo-il*) with "the Lord's Day" (*joo-il*). Early Christians replaced their Sabbath day, Saturday, with "the Lord's Day," Sunday, to mark and celebrate Jesus' resurrection. Following this tradition, Korean Christians call Sunday "the Lord's Day" to mark the act of setting apart the sacred time. However, as immigrants, Korean American Christians experience a conflict between keeping this commandment and needing to work long hours seven days a week in order to survive. Due to many factors affecting displaced people—including language barriers, racial discrimination, and little recognition of professional qualifications—many immigrants, even those who had been professionals in Korea, open up small businesses for their livelihood as soon as they have saved up enough financial resources. These small businesses, like green grocers and small convenience stores, however, work on the promise that they are open twenty-four hours a day, seven days a week. Also, in order for these businesses to profit, family labor is needed. Family members take turns around the clock working at the store. At the same time, faithful Christians are expected not only to attend worship on Sunday but also to spend the whole day at church in various meetings and events, including fellowship. So, in order for one family member to keep the Lord's Day, another has to work. Or, in some instances, they hire cheap labor of another immigrant group to keep the store open while the family observes the Lord's Day.

Creating a Sabbath in the midst of a profit- and time-driven economy is difficult and countercultural. The command to set aside a day to rest is a command for every Christian, not just for those who can afford not to work seven days a week. This command challenges us to revision a different economic society. What has to happen in order for everyone to be able to keep Sabbath? Additionally, there needs to be critical awareness and repentance, because in order for some to keep Sabbath, others have to work.

This setting apart takes on bodily significance as well—not only in terms of working and laboring but also in terms of adornment and appropriate dress. Just as we read in the Gospel about a man who was inappropriately dressed for the wedding banquet and thus thrown out (Matt. 22:11–12), Korean Americans pay particular attention to preparing the body and mind for the Lord's Day. One of the authors shares her childhood experience:

> While I was growing up in Korea, we did not have a shower in the house. Once a week, we went to a bathhouse. My grandmother always chose to do it on Saturday in order to prepare for the Lord's Day. On Saturday, she cleansed her body and made sure that her daughter-in-law washed and ironed her Sunday clothes. On Sunday, she only wore the clothes that had just been laundered. Although I never heard her say this, it appeared that it was very important not to have any blemishes in the way she presented herself to the Lord on Sunday. For my grandmother, at least on Sunday, her body became the temple in which God's spirit dwelt. For her, holiness was intimately connected to cleanliness. Preparing for the Holy required cleansing the body.

This way of preparing for the Lord's Day takes the form of honoring the body. Appropriate attire, in addition to cleanliness, adorns the body on the Lord's Day. This practice of adornment takes on a special political significance for marginalized people who have limited access to public display. On Sunday everyone, including cashiers, house cleaners, doctors, and green grocers, can all be dressed like kings and queens. For many immigrants, the public display of their full humanity created in God's image can only occur on the Lord's Day. Because of the significance of this public display, some take their adornment to the extreme and turn the Lord's Day into a fashion day. Competition for the best and the most expensive clothes and accessories further marginalizes those without the means or desire to dress in the latest fashion.

There is also another bodily aspect of this Sabbath-keeping practice that needs examination. Even among those who keep the Lord's Day, the sense of rest is hard to find. There is a saying, "A change is as good as a rest." On Sunday, Korean American Christians take a rest from their weekly work but take on another kind of work, church work. The concept of the Lord's Day for Korean Americans is not a day of rest, a Sabbath day. Korean Americans work extremely hard at church, although not for money. This is especially true for Korean American women who do the bulk of the work, though it may go unrecognized. What distinguishes the Lord's Day from a regular weekday is not rest from work but which "master" they serve, God or mammon (money).

The work that goes on in the Korean American churches is not only spiritual and Christian but also cultural. The Lord's Day is a day of claiming one's own culture for Korean American Christians. It is a day when they gather to take refuge from the harsh realities of immigrant life. They gather and speak in their own language, share in Korean meals, and regroup as a people. For the younger generation, the church offers Korean language, history, and culture classes. For the elderly and for recent immigrants, English classes are offered. Additionally, the church functions as an information center on legal and social matters important for survival. Gathering at church on Sunday provides a time and a space where different generations gather and struggle with issues of belonging and of communal and individual identities. Korean American churches, like other ethnic churches, are more than just a religious center. Churches help Korean Americans negotiate between the dominant U.S. culture and the immigrant culture. They serve both to assist Korean Americans to assimilate "Americanness" yet preserve "Koreanness" for the next generations. Although the flurries of activities are focused mainly on Sunday, other gatherings throughout the week help them not only to sustain their faith but also to be reminded that they are a part of a community.

Being part of the community necessarily requires one to keep faith practices of that community, such as Sabbath keeping and early morning prayer meetings. The Korean and Korean American faith practices seem to weigh heavily on the "right rites." Drawing on the Confucian ideology that sees that keeping the correct rites is what makes one truly human, Korean and Korean American spirituality stresses the importance of keeping certain practices. As Dorothy Bass and Craig Dykstra articulate, for Korean Americans, "just taking a full and earnest part in [practices] is somehow good in itself."[5] However, practices of a community constantly need to be critically examined to see if they can be done better. Sabbath practices of Korean Americans are an example. What can be changed in the ways the Korean Americans observe the Lord's Day if the suggestion by Dorothy Bass was taken seriously? Bass suggests how modern-day Christians can keep a sabbath holy: 1) rest from commerce; 2) rest from worry; 3) rest for creation; 4) rest from work; 5) worship.[6] Resting from commerce and worshiping is already a major part of Sabbath practices of Korean Americans. But the other three areas need to be worked on. The understanding of "holiness" also needs to be reexamined. Setting aside time to gather to worship and pray is unquestionably understood as a holy activity. However, one may need to ask, What else could be considered holy? Can political organizing to make the voices of marginalized people heard in the U.S. public arena also be considered a holy activity for the children of God? Shouldn't spirituality weave through both the religious and political aspects of our lives?

QUESTIONS FOR REFLECTION

1. What are some of your practices of keeping Sabbath? What is your sacred time and sacred space? Is the Sunday worship service the only practice of keeping Sabbath?

2. The Scripture verse "Your body is a temple of the Holy Spirit" (1 Cor. 6:19a) has often been narrowly interpreted by many Korean American Christians to mean only to purify and adorn one's body for the purpose of presenting oneself to God. This interpretation has led to a denial of the goodness of bodily experience of human life, such as sex and dancing, particularly in the context of Sabbath observance. The body as the living temple needs to be affirmed and honored. What are some ways we can do this?

3. Given the socioeconomic location of Korean Americans, what does it mean to take Dorothy Bass's suggestions of observing Sabbath seriously—for instance, Sabbath as a rest from commerce?

4. The concept and experience of "Sabbath" is different for various religious and cultural groups. Explore "Sabbath" observances of other religious/cultural groups and discuss how these encounters can mutually enhance the practice of keeping Sabbath in respective communities.

Chapter 3

Let Everything That Has Breath, Sing!

The Practice of Singing the Faith

Imagine a gathering of Christians around the world. For an informal fellowship in an evening, they all agree to have a group singing. An observer wonders, "How would it be possible to have a communal singing when they all come from such diverse backgrounds? What songs do they have in common?" To her surprise, the gathering breaks into singing, "Blowing in the Wind," "Puff the Magic Dragon," and "We Shall Overcome." They know not only the tunes, but all the words in English. Like invisible threads, somehow these 1960s songs have connected everyone gathered and created a world community.
> —from a story Su Yon heard at the Korean American Clergy
> Women PC(USA) Conference

WE ARE WHAT WE SING

Almost every living being that breathes sings. It is a universal phenomenon. Yet singing is also very particular. Thus says an African proverb, "If you want to know me, come and learn my song." Singing indeed is an important part of Korean American life. First-generation Korean Americans cannot have a good time without songs. There is almost always a lot of community singing at Korean American gatherings. It is also a common practice that everyone gathered has to sing at least one song on his or her own before the party is over. No one is exempted from performing this duty, whether one has a good voice or not. Of course, this practice certainly may be burdensome for those who do not like to sing or who cannot carry a tune. Yet as long as one wants to remain part

25

of a community, she or he must sing. Given such a context, some people will take time to learn and practice the latest Korean pop song just for these occasions. Others will sing the same song every time a group gathers. Everyone has to have at least one song that they can sing in such gatherings, and Koreans call this song *ship-pal-bun* (which literally means number eighteen, but it is considered their favorite song). As long as you have a song, you belong to the group. Everyone has a voice, and everyone is heard.

Thus, it is no surprise that singing has come to assume a very important place in the Korean American Christian community. Readily, one can hear the sanctuary being filled with the passionate singing of a congregation, regardless of the size. In most churches, members gather fifteen minutes before the Sunday morning worship to prepare themselves. They usually sing highly emotive songs at this time. Moreover, in many churches, the evening worship service is called praise worship (*chan-yang yeh-bae*). During praise worship, worshipers sing mostly contemporary gospel songs to their heart's content in a more relaxed atmosphere. The place of music ministry is indeed extremely important in the worship life of every congregation. In fact, almost every public prayer during worship makes a reference to a choir that "raises its voices to bring glory to God and to bring solace to the congregation that hears it." A vibrant music program is also considered one of the most effective evangelistic tools. Many churches invest a lot of their resources to strengthen their music ministries. They try to attract the most well-qualified musicians to provide leadership for their music ministries, and are eager to equip themselves with good musical instruments, including an organ, piano, keyboard, and percussion instruments, as well as with a good sound system. The number of churches that have an instrumental ensemble during worship is growing.

Korean American Christians know how powerful music is in their lives. This is most likely due to the Korean experience with music. Most that study Korean culture and religions agree that shamanism is at the core of Korean popular religiosity and popular culture and that Korean arts, including music and dance, developed in the crucible of shamanistic practices. In the case of the Korean shamanistic ritual called *kut*, for instance, the role of music is extremely important. Shamans dance, chant, and sing to the percussion music in order to "enter into the ecstatic state of meeting with gods and spirits."[1] In other words, it is music that mediates the connection between this world (human) and the other world (spirits/gods). Likewise, Korean American Christians consider music as a powerful spiritual resource and appropriate it to meet their needs in faithful living.

Regardless of their size, all Korean American churches have at least one choir that provides music during the morning worship service. Additionally, many Korean American churches have other choral groups that provide opportunities for their church members to practice their faith through singing. These include children's choir, youth choir, mothers' choir, male quartet, and praise teams. Big cities like Los Angeles even have other citywide choral groups that are interdenominational. One example is an elder choir, which is a male chorus. These choral groups as well as some big church choirs periodically hold concerts for the larger Korean American community, and they sometimes perform in other racial/ethnic communities, building intercultural bridges.

In fact, intercultural bridge building occurs on many levels through music, even in the practice of singing itself. Korean Americans love to sing African American spirituals, for instance, and "Lord, I Want to be a Christian" is one of our favorite hymns included in the Korean hymnal. There is something in African American spirituals that comforts and feeds the souls of Korean Americans. Perhaps it is in those spaces in the spirituals in which one just hums along meditatively or sings in nonsense syllables (unlike most of the European and American hymns that are filled with so many words for every note) that Korean Americans find their resting place in God. The bridge-building role of music in the Korean American context also can be observed in instances of worship services held jointly with other racial ethnic faith communities. Often, there is a lot more singing than spoken words, allowing more people to participate in the service across the language barrier. Singing allows people to relate on another level, creating a sense of community.

Moreover, singing allows the Korean American faith community to overcome its gender barrier to some extent. Singing in the main choir is indeed one ministry in which girls and women can participate without any gender barrier, most probably because the Western choral music we sing requires four parts, two of which are female parts. At least in the choir, there is gender equity. Since the Korean American faith community still functions as a dual-gendered system that confers leadership primarily to men, singing in the choir is an important venue through which women can assume leadership. Nevertheless, women's participation is often limited to singing the songs that are chosen by male choir directors. Almost always the church accompanist is a woman, and only in a few cases do women serve as choir directors.[2]

Music is indeed an essential element of Korean American spiritual life. Even outside the sanctuary Korean American Christians fill their lives with songs by playing hymn and gospel song tapes in the car and in their houses. In busy workplaces like grocery stores, dry cleaners, and garment factories, one can hear hymns and gospel songs being softly played all day long in the background. Many say that these holy songs purify their souls and make God's presence real to them. These songs comfort Korean American Christians and give them strength to go on living with confidence in God despite the challenges they face on a daily basis.

For Korean immigrants who experience uprootedness and alienation, these songs not only help them connect with God but also with other immigrants. If we understand a "root song" to be a song that can be sung by everyone in the community, thereby creating a sense of belonging, it would be fair to say that these hymns and gospel songs make up the root songs for the emerging Korean

American Christian community. The majority of Korean American Protestant churches share one hymnal published in 1983 by the Korean Hymnal Publication Commission represented by twenty Protestant denominations.[3] In the Foreword, one reads that this hymnal was published on the occasion of the 100th Anniversary of Korean mission as a response to a concern about divisions in the Korean Christian community. The Korean-English bilingual version of the same hymnal was published by the same commission in Korea in 1984. A point worth noting is that, with time, most Korean American churches came to use this bilingual hymnal even though a Korean-English hymnbook had already been published in the United States in 1978 at the initiative of the Korean immigrant church leadership, mostly Presbyterian.[4]

When we compare the intent stated in the Foreword and Preface of each of these two bilingual hymnals, we observe a difference in motives. The publication of the U.S. bilingual hymnal was motivated by the Korean American church leadership, which felt an increasing need to bridge the linguistic gap experienced with the emerging generation of Korean Americans for whom English was the primary language. In other words, publication of this bilingual hymnal was a self-initiated attempt on the part of the first generation to create an intergenerational community, through the practice of singing, that had a cohesive sense of identity as Korean Americans and Korean Canadians.[5]

The publication of the bilingual hymnal in Korea, on the other hand, was motivated by the leadership of the Korean church, which interpreted the need of bilingualism in immigrant churches in North America as a sign of its own growth beyond national borders. If the publication of the ecumenical hymnal in 1983 was an attempt made by the Korean Hymnal Publication Commission to bring unity across denominational divisions, publication of the Korean-English bilingual hymnal by the same commission in 1984 was an attempt to unite Korean Christians across national borders through singing.[6]

As has already been noted, the majority of Korean immigrant churches in North America use the Korean-English hymnal published in 1984; therefore, the hymns included in this hymnal make up the core music for Korean American Protestant Christian singing across the denominational lines, especially for the first generation. Korean American Protestant Christians sing these songs in any type of gathering of the faithful. We sing them in the time of praise, worship, district worship services, prayer meetings, weddings, funerals, and family worship. We even sing them in church business meetings, since our business meetings begin with prayer, Scripture reading, and hymn singing. With prayer and Scripture, singing is an integral part of any Korean gathering of the faithful, and thus very important for community building. Learning to sing these songs, therefore, is an important membership criterion in the Korean American Christian community. If we say that what we sing is who we are, it is time to explore further what Koreans Americans sing about.

HOW SHALL WE SING THE LORD'S SONG
IN A FOREIGN LAND?

"Ye-su-ro na-eh goo-joo sam-go, sung-ryung-kwa pee-ro-sseuh kuh-deup-na-nee. . . ." Singing these words with gusto with the piano accompaniment are members of a Korean American congregation. The hymn is No. 204 in the Korean hymnal, and underneath the Korean language title is written the original English title, "Blessed Assurance, Jesus Is Mine," one of the famous hymns written by F. J. Crosby in 1873. The Korean hymnal that was supposedly created to unify Korean Christians is largely a collection of hymns mostly from Europe and the United States. Many of them are the revival camp songs of nineteenth-century America.[7] Out of 558 hymns included in this hymnal, only sixteen have a Korean as their composer and lyricist. Out of these sixteen hymns, only three are composed using the traditional Korean musical modality.[8] Moreover, not a single Korean secular or folk melody appears in the hymnal whereas as many as thirty-two hymns use European secular and folk melodies.[9]

The Korean hymnal as a cultural form, then, is hardly Korean. What makes this hymnal Korean are the singers, the language we sing, and the way we sing. These hymns, though Western in form, have become beloved hymns for Korean/Korean American Christians over the years, and they continue to function powerfully as "root songs" for the Korean American Christians. They evoke memories that are uniquely Korean and Korean American, and they continue to shape and give expression to the Korean American faith experience.

Still, one cannot ignore the cultural ethos and modality of these songs when we consider the central role the Korean churches play in the context of immigrant life as a site of identity formation and cultural preservation and production. One cannot escape the critical observation that singing these Christian songs may have served as a powerful tool of acculturation in the Western tradition for Korean/Korean American Christians. By immigrating to the United States, Korean Christians, in fact, have come to the place of origin for many of the songs that are dear to their hearts. One of the authors recalls her early childhood experience:

> As a child in Korea I lived with my grandmother. Revival meetings were very popular among Korean Christians those days, and my grandmother often went to those meetings. One day, she called out my name over and over again, asking me to come and see her. When I went to her, she said, "I want you to sing this song that I learned at the revival meeting yesterday," while pointing to a paper that she had pasted on the wall. On the paper were the lyrics written by my grandmother in her very rudimentary handwriting. You know, like many other women converts to Christianity, she had learned to read and write in Korean to read the Bible and sing hymns when she converted to Christianity. Feeling a sense of superiority, I said to my grandmother, "Grandma, don't you know anything? How do you

expect me to sing these words without musical notations? Don't you know that you need to have notes to make music?" My grandmother insisted, and grew angry because I would not cooperate. Finally, I asked her to sing in the way she learned at the revival meeting. What I heard was something very akin to Korean traditional songs. Of course, I don't know if the song was actually supposed to be sung in the way she did. What I know is that she did not sing it the way that you and I sing songs these days. Now I wish I could hear her. I wish she would ask me to come and sing for her. Then I would tell her, "No, grandma, you have to sing it for me. I need to hear your song, not mine, not anybody else's." I ache to know how early Korean converts sang their songs when the Korean music was all that they knew, before they were taught that the Western music was the real music and the Western way of singing was the correct way.

In this sense, Korean immigrants were already made strangers to their tradition in their own land even before they left Korea. One may even say that those Korean Americans who came to the United States already knowing these songs had a head start in the process of assimilation to some extent. Given this, an existential question Korean Americans may need to ask themselves is, "How shall we sing the LORD's song in a foreign land?" (Ps. 137:4 RSV).

In the last three decades, there has been a resurgence of interest in recovering and/or reinventing Korean culture in South Korea. It has been an effort largely motivated and supported by the national government that tried to use culture as a medium of solidifying national unity and identity, but concerned Christian musicians in South Korea have also made various attempts to recover their lost cultural identity in their singing. Hymns and gospel songs have been written using the Korean musical modality. One composer has written a variant melody using the Korean modality for every hymn found in the current hymnal. Instruments such as *chang-gu* (drum) and *ka-ya-geum* (stringed instrument) have substituted for the organ and piano as instruments of accompaniment. These efforts have met many challenges from within the Christian communities in South Korea because of the unfortunate legacy of missionary Christianity that devalued Korean culture. Some Korean/Korean American Christians identify Korean music and instruments with popular religiosity manifest in shaman rituals; some see Korean music as not sacred because it is not Christian and not Western; and others see Korean music as simply inferior and inappropriate for church music. One of the authors recounts the following experience in Korean America:

I was visiting my grandmother who lives in a three-generation household on Long Island. Knowing that I play Korean drums, my cousin who serves as an accompanist at a church excitedly brought up the subject of drumming in the church worship. According to her, her husband, who is the conductor of the church's choir, used the Korean drum for accompaniment a couple Sundays ago, and this got several people very upset. Apparently, among those who were most upset was my grandmother. So, my cousin asked my grandmother, who was sitting around with me, "So what's wrong with playing the Korean drum for worship? You don't seem to have any problem with the drum band in the church. So, what's the difference between the drum (meaning Western) and the Korean drum?" To this, my grandmother responded very emphatically, "Korean drum is not acceptable. Everybody else has a Western drum band, but nobody does Korean drumming in the church." "Why not? What's the difference?" my cousin continued. Then my grandmother said in a rather reflective yet serious voice, "Korean drumming reminds me of the old days when I used to attend shamanistic rituals (*kut*). We cannot turn the holy sanctuary into a place where shamanistic rituals take place (*kut-dang*)."

This experience illumines the personal nature of the conflict in practicing faith. To this grandmother, conversion to Christianity meant a break with the Korean music that was connected to and reminded her of the old religion. To her, her new religious identity required that break. It illustrates the serious conflict involved in the struggle for the Korean American church to affirm its cultural roots while upholding its Christian identity.

Despite these difficulties, efforts to authenticate culturally their Christian worship have taken root in some sectors of the Christian community in South Korea, and awareness has increased as a result. However, they do not seem to have a broad-based support yet. Western music still abounds everywhere in spite of the fact that some of these emerging songs have already been incorporated in the hymnals of several global ecumenical and denominational bodies outside Korea and are being sung by people of faith around the world.[10]

Similar changes are slowly taking root in the U.S. context. A small number of concerned Korean Americans involved in music and liturgy are introducing these newly emerging songs into congregational life. Increasingly, one can see conductors choosing new songs written by Korean composers using the Korean musical modality. Yet Korean traditional songs and traditional instruments have not yet found their way into the congregational life except in a few instances.

As previously mentioned, some Korean Christians who study worship and spirituality contend that the spiritual energy of Koreans has been suppressed by the dominance of the Western culture in the Korean church context. They argue that the Korean church must take action to change its current liturgical culture in order to revive the spiritual energy of Korean Christians, and they assert that this process of reformation can begin by singing the songs that are borne out of the depth of the Korean ethos.[11] For Korean American practitioners of faith, it is time to seriously consider this challenge and begin the process of healing from our own cultural alienation by learning the rhythms of our ancestors.

Practices that have developed over time, however, are difficult to break even if they are bad practices. Besides, such awareness is not shared by many in the Korean American church context. The emerging generation is further alienated from the Korean culture. Their mode of communication is primarily English, and their English worship employs mostly the so-called contemporary gospel music.

Although the Presbyterian Church (U.S.A.) and the United Methodist Church jointly published in 2001 another bilingual hymnal[12] that is extremely multicultural and diverse in musical styles, and even includes twenty-three hymns written by Koreans and Korean Americans, with many using the Korean musical modality, the response of the Korean faith community has been minimal. This shows the difficulty involved in bringing about changes in faith practices.

POETRY OF OUR SONGS: WHAT DO WE SING ABOUT?

It has been said that Korean Christians do not pay much attention to what they sing about and that they are more interested in the "movement of the spirit they experience while singing."[13] Yet when one considers that "over time, participation in the practice of lifting their voices to God had worked in subtle and complex ways to shape basic attitudes, affections, and ways of regarding themselves, their neighbor, and God,"[14] we need to examine the content of the Korean American practice of singing.

Although civil religion is not consciously practiced in the Korean or Korean American faith context, on special Korean national holidays such as *sam-il-jul* (March First Independence Day) and *kwang-bok-jul* (Day of Liberation), one can hear the South Korean national anthem sung by the worshiping community as a closing hymn in many Korean American churches. By so doing, the first-generation Korean immigrants remember their national history of independence movement and liberation from Japanese occupation as God's story. They praise the God of history, solidify their sense of national identity, and share their deepest yearnings for the healing of the country through singing the anthem.

The above happening only occurs once or twice a year. For the rest of the year, Korean American Christians sing hymns and gospel songs, most of which are found in the hymnal described earlier. Koreans have been characterized as *han*-ridden,[15] people with a strong pathos of victimization. This pathos expresses itself most acutely in prayer meetings where people are often invited to sing the songs of their choice. Many of the songs sung in these gatherings are *han-pu-ri* songs.[16] They sing mostly about the human condition of sinfulness, Jesus' blood and crucifixion, and his salvation, and they plead for forgiveness and blessing. Through singing these favorite hymns, they bring their sorrows and pains to Jesus and weep with Jesus. They identify with the suffering Jesus.

Indeed, when one turns to the section on salvation in the hymnal, one notes that every hymn in the section has major references to sin, the blood of Jesus Christ, purification, and the cross. Nowhere in the hymnal is Jesus portrayed as a liberator. Freedom is a metaphor used only once or twice in the entire hymnal to describe the experience of salvation. The primary identity described in these songs is that of a sinner. There are only two or three songs that specifically sing about those who are sinned against. In other words, the doctrine of atonement forms the core of the belief system for Korean and Korean American Christians. In and through songs, Korean and Korean American Christians express our desire and appreciation for individual salvation and the promise of paradise. The songs we sing are privatistic and otherworldly, and often filled with the pathos of a sinner. This disengagement of collective suffering in music is puzzling because in early Christianity in Korea, Koreans identified strongly with the story of exodus. Many Christians played a key role in resisting Japanese oppression and leading the movement for liberation of Koreans from Japan, singing the song of hope and liberation.

Still, Korean American singing is not monolithic. These days, one can also hear upbeat songs at the time of praise. This time of singing is usually led by young people who prefer contemporary gospel music, and it is often accompanied by an electronic keyboard and a drum band, and is filled with joy and awe. Most of the songs have simple melodies and few words that are repeated over and over again like chants. What is interesting is that first-generation Korean men and women let go of their inhibitions and sing with body motions (*yuldong*), and in the name of praise, allow themselves to become like children and ride on the music.

Despite the joyful noise made together as a faith community, these songs seldom focus on the faith community as a whole or the faith community's struggle against injustices in the world, such as the division of Korea. This kind of singing practice may have helped heal private wounds and motivate individuals with hopes to continue their life journeys. However, one may wonder if perhaps it is these songs that have kept Korean and Korean American Christians overly inward looking and otherworldly. It is time to sing new songs that may help Korean Americans heal their wounded collective psyche and move them toward forgiveness. It is time for Korean Americans to sing new songs that give power to move beyond their divisions and toward reconciliation. Moreover, it is time for them to struggle seriously with the conflict they experience between their religious and ethnic/cultural identities and recover a sense of self that has integrity and authenticity. This does not necessarily mean that we have to give up our current practice completely. It probably is an impossible task for all Korean American Christians to learn to sing in the Korean traditional way. The medium that we use in this English-speaking North America already betrays the musicality of the Korean language and Korean music. However, we can become creators of a new liturgical culture that is rooted in the Korean ethos and the Korean American experience. God has been doing great things in the Korean peninsula since the twenty-first century dawned. Like African Americans, who through the practice of their songs during the civil rights movement were able to challenge institutional racism and the course of history, Korean Americans who love music and know its power must begin to sing new songs that empower us to release our suppressed spiritual energy and untangle our *han* so that we can dream new dreams and see new visions. Do we hear Mary's song?

And Mary said,
My soul magnifies the Lord,
and my spirit rejoices in God my Savior,
for he has looked with favor on the lowliness of his servant.
Surely, from now on all generations will call me blessed.

(Luke 1:46–48)

QUESTIONS FOR REFLECTION

1. The psalmist says, "Let everything that breathes praise the LORD!" (Ps. 150:6a). What does this phrase evoke in you?

2. What songs and/or hymns do you sing most often? What are the favorite hymns of your church community? What do these hymns sing about?

3. The hymns people sing form and reinforce their own understanding of their identity. Korean American Christians tend to sing hymns that focus on human sinfulness, suffering, and the cross—hymns that reinforce their Christian identity primarily as sinners rather than a people of resurrection. Why do you think this is the case?

4. What are the Korean American cultural elements found in the practice of hymn singing in the church? What makes these songs Korean American?

5. Do the familiar root songs of your faith community move you beyond the nostalgic past into the future of hope? What needs to change in your practice of singing to make this possible? How does the image of singing a new song in a foreign land challenge your current practice of singing?

6. The practice of singing has the potential to build bridges across lines of race, class, gender, generation, and language. Think of various ways by which such bridge making can happen in your community through singing.

Chapter 4

Fervent Prayer

The Practice of Praying Together

We were outside in the beautiful meadows up in the Poconos. At midnight, the pastor told everyone to dress warmly to go out to pray. We had to pray out loud for one hour. And if we could not pray, he told us to recite the Lord's Prayer over and over until our own prayer took hold of our voices. Obediently, I, along with thirty other college students, knelt in the wet grass and looked up at the stars. I tried to pray out loud, but nothing would come out. Being bilingual, I did not know whether to pray in Korean or in English. So, as the pastor told us, I recited the Lord's Prayer in Korean. I must have been reciting it for about ten minutes. Suddenly, my own prayer took voice and I was praying prayers I did not know were inside me. I was praying, like Jacob, to bless me and to make God known to me. I was yelling at God, that I was not going to leave this mountain without God's blessing. Around me were other voices, rising together in the night. Some were singing, others were crying, and others shaking fists in anger to God. I wrestled with God in a loud voice for about an hour. And suddenly, I felt this peace and an inner knowledge that I was a child of God. I recalled the verse from Isaiah, "I have called you by your name. You are mine." I heard the pastor singing a hymn. This was a signal that we should begin to finish our prayers and join him in the hymn. I looked up into the sky, and the stars were so beautiful. For the first time, I knew the stars were shining for me.

—from Su Yon's prayer journal

TONG-SUNG KI-DO (CRYING OUT IN ONE VOICE)

Tong-sung ki-do, which literally means "praying together out loud," is a unique Korean/Korean American practice of faith. Those gathered offer individual prayers aloud, simultaneously, in the context of the faith community. It is unique because as a public form of prayer it is individualized and yet collective. It can also be practiced privately as an individual *tong-sung ki-do*. Whether practiced in private or in community, *tong-sung ki-do* is offered in a loud voice.

On the one hand, this prayer is a way of laying down the burden of the agony, emotional displacement, oppression, discrimination, and frustration of immigrant life. On the other hand, this practice is an empowering synergy of different tones and voices and distinct intentions. Pray-ers may come together for *tong-sung ki-do* for a variety of reasons: some to lament, some for emotional catharsis, some for discernment, some to confess, and some to demand God's intervention in their lives. Regardless of the reason, each person's prayer is borne heavenward on the wave of the surrounding prayers. It is a clear outward testimony to the presence of a personal and living faith among Korean American Christians. More broadly, in this practice of faith Korean American Christians preserve and value the universal Christian tradition of extemporaneous prayer in worship.

Tong-sung ki-do has the character of a visceral struggle with God. Like Jacob wrestling with the angel, *tong-sung ki-do* is a form of wrestling with God. The wrestling is not just emotional and spiritual, but also physical. *Tong-sung ki-do* is an embodied prayer. The kneeling, rocking back and forth, hands moving up and down, voices rising, and hitting the ground with a fist are all body movements that accompany prayer. In fact, it is so physical that if the body is not accustomed to praying in this way, one cannot pray long before all sensation is lost in the legs. It requires the discipline of the body as well as the mind. To intensify the physicality of the prayer, some pray holding onto a tree all night, sometimes even progressively uprooting it. Wrestling with a tree as one wrestles with God testifies that prayer is an act of physical labor.

There is no one way of praying the *tong-sung ki-do*. But there are certain patterns one can observe. Individual *tong-sung ki-do* may take place in a church sanctuary, either early in the morning or late at night when no one is around. Some choose to pray underneath the cross; some choose a corner of the sanctuary. What is important is that whichever place they choose, it must have some significance. The location of the cross may give a sense of being closer to Jesus and his suffering. It may also have a symbolic meaning of offering one's own self, body and mind, as a sacrifice. But some feel that they cannot pray near the cross since the cross is usually in the "altar" area, and particularly some women feel that they are not worthy to pray in the "holy" place where the ordained pastors and elders preach and read the Scripture. They may choose a corner of the sanctuary, but with a full view of the cross.

As an alternative to the church sanctuary, individuals may go up to the prayer house (*ki-do-won*) to pray intentionally about a particular issue. Pastors and leaders of the church regularly practice this as a way of redirecting their spiritual energies and/or to pray about particular difficulties in their congregations, such as lack of members or lack of spiritual focus. These prayer houses, which are similar to retreat centers, are located in the mountains or in a quiet countryside. They have a set schedule that individuals can follow: early morning worship, daytime meditation on the Scripture, and evening worship. The program is usually over around 10:00 p.m. Then individuals go outside in the mountain for *tong-sung ki-do*, which can last all night.

As a public collective prayer, *tong-sung ki-do* has a place in early morning prayer services, regular Sunday service, revival meetings, and group prayer meetings. Although prayed individually, yet together in the same place and same time, the *tong-sung ki-do* may have a collective theme. Common in the collective *tong-sung ki-do* are receiving the Holy Spirit, discovering God's will, raising funds for church building, Korean reunification, healing, and the pastor's leadership. The congregants know to start their prayers when they hear the leader praying in a loud voice. The leader's voice also signals the end of the prayer, which gets softer and sometimes ends in the singing of a well-known hymn, like "Amazing Grace," where everyone eventually joins in. The leader will usually end with a prayer on behalf of everyone to close the *tong-sung ki-do*. During revival meetings, a charismatic revival preacher may go around to each of the congregants and lay hands on their heads and pray (*an-su ki-do*). This is to encourage the pray-er in the concerted effort and to impart a special blessing. The charismatic revivalists are usually renowned for their preaching and their spiritual power. So, receiving the *an-su ki-do* from them is seen as a tremendous privilege and a gift of strength for the spiritual journeys of the congregants.

> Are any among you suffering? They should pray. Are any cheerful? They should sing songs of praise. Are any among you sick? They should call for the elders of the church and have them pray over them, anointing them with oil in the name of the Lord. The prayer of faith will save the sick, and the Lord will raise them up; and anyone who has committed sins will be forgiven. . . . Elijah was a human being like us, and he prayed fervently that it might not rain. . . . Then he prayed again, and the heaven gave rain. (James 5:13–15, 17a, 18a)

It is intriguing how Koreans/Korean Americans came to practice such a unique form of prayer. In our earlier discussion of the social history of the Korean American church in the United States, we noted that group consciousness results from experiencing historical events of significance. *Tong-sung ki-do*, as a unique form of prayer practiced by Korean Americans, is not unrelated to the historical experience shared by them as a people.

HISTORICAL EXPERIENCE OF KOREAN IMMIGRANTS

One cannot fully understand *tong-sung ki-do* without the actual historical context from which the practice rose. At least four recent historical markers shape identity and religious expression for Korean immigrants: Japanese colonization (1909–1945), the Korean War (1950–1953), political unrest during oppressive military dictatorship (1961–1992), and immigration.

During Japanese colonization, the language, the culture, the land, and the essence of being Korean was robbed from Koreans. On a daily basis they experienced being despised, mocked, and discriminated against, and their survival depended on their silence and their ability to resist and endure. Just as the psalmist cried out, "My God, my God, why have you forsaken me? . . . But I am a worm, and not human; scorned by others, and despised by the people" (Ps. 22:1–6a), Koreans also were treated like worms.

The period of Japanese colonization ended in 1945, only soon to be followed by the division of the peninsula by the Soviet and U.S. military. Then a civil war ensued through which families experienced catastrophe in very personal ways. Brothers were either abducted into the military or voluntarily joined the army of either side, never to be seen again. Death separated families. Ideological differences tore families apart. Displacement from ancestral homes and loss of land all culminated in a permanent division of the Korean land and people. In addition to this personal suffering, the war devastated the country and its ability to provide basic life sustenance for its people. Poverty, hunger, social dislocation, and political instability added to the personal suffering that the people experienced. This political event of war brought on staggering hardship for Korean people that still lingers on in the lives of many Korean Americans. A second-generation Korean American woman recalls telling her mother, who saves every scrap of food from the meal so that it will be used later and not be wasted, "Mom, the war is over." But in reality, the war is not over for many Korean Americans. The memory of war still haunts the daily lives of many older, first-generation Korean Americans, and it is compounded by fighting the daily war of racism and discrimination in American society. Furthermore, those who have families separated between North and South Korea continue to live with the pain of not knowing what happened to their loved ones on the other side of the division, holding on to a sliver of hope to be reunited with them one day.

In addition to colonization and war, the seemingly perpetual state of division on the Korean peninsula left the legacy of thirty-two years of military government in South Korea, which exacerbated the traumas of ideological divide and personal loss felt among Koreans. During the military dictatorship, Korean people lived in a culture of fear where anyone suspected of communist sympathies or leftist leanings was arrested or executed, all in the name of national security. The government maintained itself on propaganda and fear. In this climate, certain people were targeted for anti-government activities. These included activists, intelligentsia, religious leaders, and especially college students and factory laborers. The government restricted activities such as freedom of speech and freedom of assembly. The people experienced mistrust, lack of agency, and rampant corruption causing powerlessness in their daily life. One of the aspects of life lived under military dictatorship was a curfew between midnight and 4:00 in the morning. Curfew was a practice that started during Japanese colonization and continued through the Korean War and military dictatorship. After midnight, Korean people's outside activities were prohibited. At 4:00 in the morning, the curfew was lifted. It was only then that the people were free to move around and gather. For this reason, dawn evoked many meanings for the Korean people as a symbol of awakening and returning to life.

Finally, experiences of immigration, especially since 1965, have been a significant historical marker in the experience of Korean Americans. Korean immigrants brought with them the suffering they experienced from the history of Korea. In addition to this, they experienced the trauma of immigrant life, which consisted of long and hard labor, social dislocation, discrimination, cultural and language barriers, racism, and anti-immigrant sentiments. Immigration also disrupted family life. The traditional family structure was bent under the heavy weight of the realities of immigrant life. Many women became the "rice-winners,"[1] and children, the leaders and interpreters, both linguistic and cultural, for their parents in the confusion of American society. There were also tensions between the generations. Between the immigrant first generation and the second generation, language and cultural barriers emerged, creating difficult family dynamics. Parents and children could no longer understand or talk with one another. It is in this context of suffering that *tong-sung ki-do* came to be practiced by Korean American Protestant Christians.

TONG-SUNG KI-DO AS A LAMENT

My eyes are spent with weeping;
  my stomach churns;
my bile is poured out on the ground
  because of the destruction of my people,
because infants and babes faint
  in the streets of the city.

They cry to their mothers,
  "Where is bread and wine?"
as they faint like the wounded
  in the streets of the city,
as their life is poured out
  on their mothers' bosom.
(Lam. 2:11–12)

Tong-sung ki-do as a form of lament draws its inspiration consciously or unconsciously from biblical laments, more specifically, from the laments of the book of Lamentations. The book is a series of poems articulating the anguish of the survivors of the Babylonian invasion in 587 B.C.E. Koreans and Korean Americans are instinctively drawn to interesting parallels between the book of Lamentations and their own experience. The poems in Lamentations tell the story of the survivors' attempts to make sense of war, misery, and devastating famine. In the same way, this struggle for physical survival is a visceral reality for the generation of Koreans/Korean Americans who lived through the Japanese invasion, the Korean War, the division of land, military dictatorship, and subsequent immigrations to other parts of the world. Like the poets of Lamentations, Koreans and Korean Americans use *tong-sung ki-do* to shout out their despair and demand that God do something to alleviate their suffering. *Tong-sung ki-do* is a way of making God accountable to God's covenant and promises. Reciprocally, human beings also have a part to play in this drama. We are accountable to have faith and trust and to actively cry out in this way in order to receive God's blessings. Here, each party has a responsibility to act in ways appropriate to their being and nature.

Dehumanization characterized the historical experience of Koreans during the Japanese colonial era. Like the Hebrews in exile, Korean Christians cried out of deep despair, "Why are you so far from helping me, from the words of my groaning?" (Ps. 22:1b). In this context of being silenced and oppressed, *tong-sung ki-do* was an act of resistance, a breaking of the imposed silence. *Tong-sung ki-do* was sometimes the only way to cry out about their agony and pain and was an urgent demand for God to take their side. In this way, *tong-sung ki-do* became a psychological catharsis in which the people could freely express their agony before God, and it provided a way of being released from the burden of their oppression. It also served them as a way to gather up new strength to go on living with new hopes.

In the same way that *tong-sung ki-do* functioned to release the pain of the suffering of colonization, it functioned to untangle Korean people's *han*[2] from the war and its subsequent division. *Han* is a Korean way to express the depth of human suffering. The practice of *tong-sung ki-do* has continued to operate as a testimony to the war's atrocity and devastation and its effect on future generations. After a long, dark night, the church bells rang at 4:00 a.m. as the curfew lifted, signaling a new awakening. Since the people were then free to gather, it was then that Korean Christians came together for *tong-sung ki-do*. Prayers began at 4:30 a.m. Given the social restriction of a curfew, one might say that the participants of the dawn prayer meetings were practicing a resistance to being exiled in their own land. The pain of these social restrictions, at times overwhelming, could be released within this prayer practice of *tong-sung ki-do*, which provided both occasion and place for people to gather.[3]

Again, given this context of suffering, *tong-sung ki-do* has served as a way of pouring out one's frustrations, anger, pain, and confusion. *Tong-sung ki-do* as a faith practice, however, is not only an emotional release. It is a faith testimony that even in the midst of the tremendous sufferings, historical and ever present, we will not be defeated. It is a cry to God demanding that God intervene and alleviate the suffering.

TONG-SUNG KI-DO AS A PASSIONATE FAITH PRACTICE

The Israelites groaned under their slavery, and cried out. Out of the slavery their cry for help rose up to God. God heard their groaning, and God remembered his covenant with Abraham, Isaac, and Jacob. God looked upon the Israelites, and God took notice of them.

(Exod. 2:23b–25)

In his anguish he prayed more earnestly, and his sweat became like great drops of blood falling down on the ground.

(Luke 22:44)

The Scripture passages above are commonly used in *tong-sung ki-do* services to connect the community to the embodied and passionate nature of this ritual practice. As the Israelites cried out to God in their oppression, Korean Americans cry out to God to remember God's covenant through Abraham, Isaac, and Jacob. As Jesus prayed earnestly, so does the church community.

The purpose of *tong-sung ki-do* may at times be very specific. When it is not used as a general lament against suffering, it may be a practice used for discernment. The discernment can be about life choices such as vocation, human relationships, and marriage, as well as about personal spiritual journeys, such as discerning the gifts and filling of the Holy Spirit.

It is also a practice of confession. First, *tong-sung ki-do* can function as a statement of contrition for one's sin and an assurance that sins are forgiven. The *tong-sung ki-do* often begins with the confession of individual sin. At other times repentance is the total focus of the practice. Second, *tong-sung ki-do* can function as a confession in the sense of being a testimony to one's faith. The fervor, the length, the embodied intensity, the loudness of the prayer all signify the depth of one's faith.

In a cultural and religious context where women's voices are often silenced, *tong-sung ki-do* gives voice to everyone. In fact, women participate in *tong-sung ki-do* more than men. It gives voice to their otherwise silent sufferings and can thus be seen as a way of surviving that which is too much to bear. But beyond survival, it is also a form of resistance. In the evangelical language of many Korean

American Christians, participating in *tong-sung ki-do* resists the power of Satan to control and to defeat the forces that produce suffering. Also, by giving voice equally to women and men, *tong-sung ki-do* is a channel through which women can pour out the suffering caused by sexism within Korean American society.

While *tong-sung ki-do* is a positive practice that promotes self-empowerment and spiritual well-being, it has its limitations and even a counterproductive side. Though it is a form of resistance to gender oppression, it rarely functions to challenge the structures of gender hierarchy that are at the root of Korean American women's experience. In this specific instance, *tong-sung ki-do* as a practice is spiritualized, cloaking the deeply expressed resistance so as to strip it of any political force that challenges structural inequalities. In fact, for many Korean American Christians, its practice may become a psychological and spiritual crutch that gives temporary relief but no lasting structural change.

Additionally, while faithful wrestling with God is its goal, *tong-sung ki-do* runs the danger of becoming only a wager of false pride. The goal then becomes receiving a concrete answer that is predetermined by the pray-er, as opposed to a discernment process in which the will of God and human need engage each other faithfully and fruitfully.

Another problem with the way *tong-sung ki-do* is practiced is its implicit demand for magical solutions to all problems. For example, a woman suffering from violence in the home may pray for help to endure the beatings or for it simply to end. But the prayer may not incorporate the critical analysis necessary to address the wider social realities that allow violence to go on or the need for the woman to pull resources together to leave the situation. The magic hoped for is, of course, a happy, united household where there is peace.

Not all Korean American Christians practice *tong-sung ki-do*. For some, *tong-sung ki-do* is an irrational, loud, shamanistic practice that brings out emotions in prayer that are unnecessary. They say, "God is not deaf; there is no need to shout." They also bring up the example of the ritualistic public prayers of the Pharisees in which Jesus took no delight. However, this critique may miss the power of *tong-sung ki-do* as a practice that can lead to both personal and social transformation.

This practice of lamentation can function to untangle the oppressive forces (communal and social *han*) that are at the root of spiritualized individual *han*. *Tong-sung ki-do* can be used as a form of social protest against specific issues that oppress and discriminate against the Korean American community. For instance, if we took *tong-sung ki-do* out of the captivity of church and into the public square, it would provide a more significant Korean American voice. What would it look like to have issues related to immigration pressed in the public forum through a fervent and embodied prayer form as well as through the political process? Like the Million Man March that brought attention to issues in the African American community, the Korean American community could organize a Million Pray-er *Tong-sung Ki-do* service outside the White House to demand attention to the effects of immigration law in the Korean American community. Can you imagine one million people praying *tong-sung ki-do* in an organized and peaceful way, but with fervor and passion? Using this practice, the Korean American community could protest immigration issues in a holistic way that incorporates their religious and their political selves.

One radical extension of this innovative use of the practice of *tong-sung ki-do* might lie in its potential for bridging race relations between Korean Americans and African Americans. Both cultures share a practice of fervent prayer in response to personal and social suffering. Participating in one another's fervent prayer practice could create a common language and experience of pleading to God and to public authorities. If both communities come to God in the same manner, it has the potential to bond them together. How might the L.A. uprising have had a different outcome if both sides had come together in wailing lament and demanded justice at the injustice of the Rodney King verdict?

As a significant practice of Korean American Christians, *tong-sung ki-do* needs to be reaffirmed as a faith practice of both spiritual and political resistance. It is an indigenous faith practice of liberation that must be released from its spiritualized captivity in the churches. By embracing its potential for collective and social outcry against oppressive political realities, *tong-sung ki-do* will become an empowering resource that couples and unites the sacred and the secular experiences of the Korean American community, thus releasing unprecedented transforming power.

QUESTIONS FOR REFLECTION

1. What are some of your experiences of suffering? Fervent prayer can be understood as a form of lament. Why do you think lament is necessary? What are some of your practices of lament?

2. Do you pray fervently? How? For instance, do you designate a time and place to pray? Do you assume a certain posture? Do you pray out loud? Do you pray alone or with other people? What situations prompt you to pray fervently? What difficulties have you experienced in fervent prayer?

3. Some people evoke the image of the God of Jacob when they are wrestling with a problem in their lives. Others evoke the image of a merciful God when they are asking for forgiveness. The images you hold onto in your prayers are often a form of testimony of your encounters with God. When you pray, what are some of the images of God that you rely on? List them. Are there any categories that emerge from your list?

4. Is it possible to imagine a religious practice so significant that it has potential to affect world events? One example might be Operation Desert Fox—the four-day bombing of Iraq, Dec. 16–19, 1998. The bombing was halted the day before the month of Ramadan in respect for Muslim religious observance. Is there space for the Korean American practice of fervent prayer in public life? If so, when and in what ways?

Chapter 5

Resourcing the Life Circle

The Practice of Re-membering
the Generations Before

> *My grandmother keeps on telling my mother that she would rather be*
> *buried in the Rose Hill Memorial Garden where the* Young-nak *Presby-*
> *terian Church owns a huge lot for its members who have crossed over to*
> *the other side. My mom says, "Mother, the lot we have prepared for you is*
> *almost right next to your son-in-law's. Don't you know that it would make*
> *it a lot easier for your children and grandchildren to come and see you if*
> *you were next to him than in Rose Hill, which is so far away [from For-*
> *est Lawn in Glendale]?" My grandmother does not budge at my mother's*
> *words of persuasion. She says, "Oh, the lot you have bought for me in For-*
> *est Lawn is so expensive. If you sold it and bought another lot for me in*
> *Rose Hill, which is so much cheaper, you will have some money left for*
> *yourself. Besides, if I am buried in Rose Hill, I hear that on the August*
> *Moon Day (Chu-sok), the* Young-nak *church folks hold an annual joint*
> *memorial service (kong-dong chu-do yeh-bae) for its members who are*
> *buried there. I think that will be wonderful." My grandmother is now*
> *buried in Rose Hill, along with her church friends who have gone before*
> *and after her.*
>
> —from Unzu's retelling of a conversation with her grandmother

Dying well has traditionally been a serious concern for Koreans. Dying well
for many Korean Americans has to do not only with how they die but also with
what happens to them after their death. One's afterlife involves what living survivors do for a deceased person. Knowing very well the immigrant situation,
where it is becoming increasingly difficult for survivors to come and visit their
family members who have passed on, this wise grandmother in the vignette chose

the church family over her biological family to remember her and take care of her after her death. She died well with an assurance that she will be memorialized at least once a year by her church family.

HYO-DO (PRACTICING FILIAL PIETY) TO BE FULLY HUMAN

Chu-sok (August Moon Day) is a three-day holiday for Koreans. It is a holiday for the harvest festival that falls on the fifteenth day of August according to the lunar calendar. Historically, as people of an agrarian society, Koreans revered the heavens and held nationwide festivals of unity in the season of harvest. The festivities involved community celebrations with drinking, eating, singing, dancing, and playing communal games. They gave an opportunity to people to appreciate the goodness of life and helped solidify the social solidarity among people from all sectors of the society. An integral part of these festivities included *che-sa* (rite of veneration) to the heavens in thanksgiving for a good year.[1] They believed that practicing this rite to the heavens promised the nation's prosperity for another year.

Rooted in this age-old tradition, Koreans, young and old, would traditionally get dressed in fine clothes on *Chu-sok* and come together as families and communities to participate in the festivities, enjoying the feasts prepared with the newly harvested crop. On this day, even women, most of whom lived very restricted lives, were given permission to enjoy freedom. They celebrated life as a community of women by dancing *Kang-kang-su-wol-lae* (women's circle dance) in the moonlight.

However, in today's practice, what characterizes this special holiday the most is paying respect to ancestors through *sung-myo* (visitation of ancestral graves) and *che-sa* (rite of veneration to their ancestors). A massive migration back home happens on this day in South Korea, where many people from farming and fishing villages have migrated to industrial centers in search of employment. The sons and daughters return home not only to their surviving parents but also to their ancestors buried in home ground.

Home, for Koreans, is ultimately the place where their family's ancestors are buried. In gratitude for the life they have received from their ancestors, the surviving descendants clean up their grave sites, set a ritual table with food and drink before the graves, pay obeisance to the ancestors by making bows, and invite the ancestors to the ritual table. Memorializing ancestors through such ritual practices is indeed an integral part of *Chu-sok* celebration that helps Korean families resource the life circle that connects everyone, both the living and the dead, in social solidarity.

Koreans have traditionally believed that there are four essential rites of passage one has to go through in order to complete the life cycle: the rite of coming of age, the rite of marriage, the rite of funeral and mourning, and the rite of veneration to ancestors. As one can see, two rites, coming of age and marriage, happen while one is living; but the other two, funeral and mourning and ancestor veneration, occur after one has died. The first two are the rites of passage that one has to goes through while living, but the other two are the rites that his/her descendants have to practice on their behalf once one has died. Yet these latter two rites are considered to be part of one's own life cycle.

This traditional understanding of a life cycle sheds some light on the perspective on life and death that is particular to the Korean cultural framework. In this perspective, death is not an end of life. Rather, death is one of the stages of a life cycle, and that life continues on after death. However, in this perspective, in order for one to continue to live well after death, one has to die well, and dying well requires living well.

In this framework, living well entails growing into adulthood (rite of coming of age) and getting married (rite of marriage) to give birth to a new generation of life (especially sons). Dying well entails meeting death at a mature age without much suffering and in the presence of descendants around the deathbed so that the descendants can give a proper funeral after death and offer *che-sa* in the years and generations to come.

This understanding is probably connected to our traditional belief that life is lived in two different realms: this world (*i-seung*) and the other/next world (*chu-seung*). In this perspective, one's life consists of life in this world and life in the next world. One does not simply go away from the living when one dies. Rather, one continues to stay connected to the living in this world through the rites of memorialization even after death, and these rites enable the dead to live well in the next world because only then does the person who has passed on fully achieve the status of an ancestor. Given this perspective, one's life after death depends on how one dies and how he or she is treated by descendants after his or her death. Furthermore, one's responsibility to care for parents does not and cannot end with their death, but has to continue even after their death.

The concept of ancestor veneration has been part of the Korean consciousness from early on.[2] However, this kind of worldview on life and death was solidified and systematized into institutionally codified practices during the five hundred years of the Yi dynasty (1392–1910) that adopted the philosophy of neo-Confucianism as its political ideology for governance.[3] As an age-old philosophy that originated in East Asia by observing natural laws that govern life, Confucianism saw that no one can be fully human in isolation because no one is self-generated. Confucianism thus asserted that one's heaven-mandated human nature can be realized only in relation to others. *In* (仁),[4] which is regarded as one of the essential characteristics of the heavenly principle and the defining attribute for human nature is, as an ideograph, made up of two humans. Thus, etymologically *in* means "co-humanity."[5] Hence, Confucianism taught that *in* should serve as the ultimate social principle for humans. In this perspective,

Confucianism asserted that because life comes from parents and the parent-child relationship is one of the most primary relationships for everyone, children can begin to cultivate *in* in relation to others including siblings, partners, friends, teachers, and nation by first practicing filial piety (*hyo*) to their parents.

Confucianism also taught that filial piety (*hyo*) has to be practiced not only when parents are living but also after they have died. Mencius, a Chinese Confucian scholar, even said, "Keeping one's parents when they are alive is not worth being described as of major importance; it is treating them decently when they die that is worth such a description."[6] Many rituals developed in the practice of filial piety (*hyo*) for the dead parents, and among them, ancestor veneration ritual (*che-sa*) became very central, almost a standard for filial piety (*hyo*), in the life of Korean families. The rite developed elaborate details, and it has been annually conducted not only on parents' memorial day (*kee-il*), which is the day of death, but also on many other days like the August Moon Day (*Chu-sok*).

Therefore, Koreans understood that it is the responsibility of the living to assure a good life for those who have passed on to the next world. In the same vein, it has been believed that ancestors who have passed on will continue to watch over and bless their descendants and protect them from misfortune in this world. In other words, the reciprocal relationship continues on, completing the life circle. There is a continuous giving and taking from one another. It is for this reason that children took great care to provide the best for their ancestors who have passed on, especially in the selection of the burial site. In this context, having all of their children at the deathbed was considered a great blessing, and by contrast, dying alone on the road was considered one of the most tragic misfortunes in one's life. Even today, this practice of being present with their parents at the time of their death is taken very seriously by first-generation Korean Americans. Likewise, one's absence at the deathbed of his or her parent is considered a serious failure to practice filial duties (*pul-hyo*), a cardinal sin.

Given this ethos, it is critical that we include this perspective in our efforts to understand the psychic trauma suffered by the separated families, altogether ten million Koreans out of thirty million at the time of division fifty years ago, because of the division of the Korean peninsula.[7] "Mother, please forgive your unfilial son!" cried out a seventy-year-old son in South Korea when he found out that his 109-year-old mother was still surviving in North Korea and that he had been selected to be one of the one hundred Koreans in the South to visit their family in the North on August 15, 2000, the day of Korean liberation.[8] His response is most typically Korean when one considers that in Korean society one is not defined as a disparate entity, but in relation to someone else, especially in relation to one's parents, and that filial piety is considered a highest virtue. In the fifty-plus years of separation, he could not have been fully human from this perspective because he could not and did not practice his filial duties.[9]

In this respect, many early Korean converts to Christianity may have understood Jesus as a perfect example of the most filial son because he obeyed his father's will unto death. Family is very important for anyone in any culture, but in such a context family takes on another layer of meaning, and consequently, how one practices one's faith in the context of family life also takes on a different shape and form.

RE-MEMBERING THOSE WHO HAVE CROSSED OVER

Children, obey your parents in the Lord, for this is right. "Honor your father and mother"—this is the first commandment with a promise: "so that it may be well with you and you may live long on the earth."

(Eph. 6:1–3)

You shall have no other gods before me. You shall not make for yourself an idol, whether in the form of anything that is in heaven above, or that is on the earth beneath, or that is in the water under the earth. You shall not bow down to them or worship them; for I the LORD your God am a jealous God, punishing children for the iniquity of parents, to the third and fourth generation of those who reject me, but showing steadfast love to the thousandth generation of those who love me and keep my commandments.

(Deut. 5:7–10)

Pastor, I called you because there is something you must know. One of the church members is still practicing an ancestor veneration ritual (che-sa). I may not have called you if he is just any member. He is an ordained leader in the church. How can we let him continue that kind of sinful practice?

—a story retold by Unzu

The ancestor veneration ritual (*che-sa*) has been a point of contention for practicing Christians ever since Christianity was introduced to Korea, and it remains an issue for Korean Americans today. In fact, many early Christian converts in Korea were persecuted, even executed by the state, for refusing to practice the ancestor veneration rites (*che-sa*).[10] Although many Korean Christians rejected *che-sa* as "ancestor spirit worship" or "idol worship"[11] that is forbidden by the first and second commandments, some have continued to practice it as a traditional expression of filial piety for parents who have passed away. Regardless, many Korean Christians still hold filial piety as a sacred duty, and it is preached often from the pulpit, using passages such as Ephesians 6:1–3. Even those Christians who have stopped practicing ancestor veneration rites in the traditional sense gather around the grave sites on the August Moon Day (*Chu-sok*) and hold a family worship service in memory of those who have already passed on. Such ceremonial remembering does not happen only on *Chu-sok*. Every year, Korean Christians hold a memorial worship service (*chu-do yeh-bae*) for many of their family members, especially the elders on their memorial day (*kee-il*), which is the day they died. Family members and friends of the dead are invited to the memorial service (*chu-do yeh-bae*), and the pastor of the church where the family holds membership is usually invited to lead the service.

On *kee-il*, the family usually places a framed picture of the one being memorialized on a table, along with some flowers. The liturgy of the memorial service is usually determined by the one leading the worship, except for one or two hymns. Hymns are usually chosen from the favorite hymns of the one being memorialized. The liturgy follows a simple pattern of opening prayer, hymn, prayer, Scripture reading, sermon, and hymn, and ends with the Lord's Prayer or benediction. A table fellowship usually follows the memorial service.[12]

During the memorial service and table fellowship, stories about the one who is being memorialized are shared among the gathered, and by so doing, those who have passed on are remembered into the community of the living. However, there is something very unique in the way the dead are remembered. The wrongdoing of the person is not remembered. By granting unconditional forgiveness to the dead, their misdeeds are erased from family and community memory, and they are re-membered into the community of saints. Thus, the living begin a renewed relationship with those who have passed on. This practice of re-membering demands some critique, however. From the perspective of the wronged, the victim, the community's demand for unconditional forgiveness of the perpetrator of suffering may be experienced as revictimization without any due recourse for justice. At the same time, it could be also understood as another way of resolving conflicts, one way of putting an end to a distorted relationship and thereby liberating the victim/survivor from the power of the abuser.

As is true in every culture, death is a very serious communal event for Koreans. Korean churches in Korea, in particular, typically have a committee of volunteers called *sang-rye-bu* that takes care of every aspect of the ritual process, which involves mourning, funeral service, and burial. In the past, when there were not many funeral homes available, these volunteers used to take care of embalmment and make the mourning clothes for members of the family that have experienced death. The family members of the dead person were traditionally required to keep watch until burial and could therefore not take care of the business themselves. Even though the United States presents a different context, and church members no longer need to assume so much responsibility in times of death as they used to in Korea, death is a serious community concern for Korean American Christians. Wakes, funerals, and burial services are usually attended by a large number of Korean Americans. Instead of bringing flowers, many bring a monetary gift to the funeral to help defray the costs involved, continuing the custom carried over from Korea. One difference that can be observed in the funeral custom in the United States is that Korean Americans tend to wear black instead of white, which is the traditional color for mourning in the Korean context.

Every year since death, many Korean American Christian families continue the practice of memorializing those who have passed on through worship and table fellowship on *kee-il*, although its annual practice is becoming increasingly difficult because of the reality of dispersion in the family. In the Korean American context, where the rhythm of life is different from Korea, many tend to choose to practice their *Chu-sok* ritual on either Thanksgiving Day or Memorial Day or both. However, some continue to observe the *Chu-sok* according to the lunar calendar. Moreover, more than individual families engage in this practice. Taking on an alternate concept of family—anyone who is in Christ is a brother or sister—some Korean American churches hold a memorial service on the Saturday closest to the *Chu-sok* for all of their church members who have passed on. Many of these churches are big churches that have the capacity to purchase a huge burial lot in memorial gardens for their members. In such cases, the pastors of the church routinely conduct a memorial service for all of its members buried in its church lot at the site on this day.

The practice of memorializing is certainly not uniquely Korean. However, one can see something very deliberate in the Korean and Korean American practice. These days, the Korean American community is much more conscious of the ardent efforts that Korean adoptees are making in search of their biological parents in Korea. Knowing where one comes from is a basic human need for one's survival in any culture. Regular memorializing allows descendants to realize where they come from and where they will go, and it solidifies family unity. Some churches, in fact, use the memorial service on the August Moon Day as an occasion to teach emerging generations about the importance of remembering and honoring ancestors. This is important for Korean Americans who live their lives disconnected from their extended families in Korea and who may sometimes feel like nobodies in a strange land. It also allows the family and church family to deal with the reality of death on a regular basis, and it provides opportunities for them to continue to work for each other's healing. Regular memorializing allows opportunities for the descendants to learn in a concrete way about the Korean value of filial piety and the value of dying well. It also allows them to learn about ancestors whom they may not have met in their lifetimes, and to build relationships between generations even after death. By so doing, the dead are not forgotten; they are re-membered into the community of the living. Also, the living become assured that they too will be taken care of when they die. This re-membering allows those who have passed on to continue to resource the life circle of the living and vice versa.

RETURNING HOME: HOPING FOR
A NEW LIFE IN PARADISE

For the wages of sin is death, but the free gift of God is eternal life in Christ Jesus our Lord.

(Rom. 6:23)

"Do not let your hearts be troubled. Believe in God, believe also in me. In my Father's house there are many dwelling places. If it were not so, would I have told you that I go to prepare a place for you? And if I go and prepare a place for you, I will come again and will take you to myself, so that where I am, there you may be also. And you know the way to the place where I am going."

(John 14:1–4)

It is true that Koreans have traditionally believed that life does not end with death, but rather continues on in spirit after death. Still, Koreans have neither glorified death nor taken it lightly. In fact, life in the next world used to be understood as a harsh reality, never as good as life in this world. Longevity, therefore, has been considered an ultimate blessing, and the untimely death of a parent an evidence of the children's failure to practice filial piety. Even if one's parent died at a mature age after a long life, children took his or her death as an evidence of their failure to practice filial piety, and some who lived by strict rites used to carry out the ritual of mourning for as many as three years.

Most Korean American Protestant Christians have moved away from such traditional perspectives on life and death. However, filial piety is still highly valued, and taking care of one's parents is still considered an obligation for children because lives in each generation are all connected in the larger life circle. Most Korean American Protestant Christians do not believe that they can make a difference in someone else's destiny after his or her death and that heaven is prepared only for those redeemed by the saving grace of Jesus Christ. Yet they still have a great interest in what happens to them and their parents after death. As believers of Jesus' teachings, they consider heaven as their original home (*pon-hyang*). Dying well means returning to the original home. Thus, in their approach to death, they strive continuously not to falter in their path. Everyone hopes to say at the end of one's life, "I have fought the good fight, I have finished the race, I have kept the faith. From now on there is reserved for me the crown of righteousness, which the Lord, the righteous judge, will give me on that day, and not only to me but also to all who have longed for his appearing" (2 Tim. 4:7–8). This probably is why they also try so hard to convert all members of the family to Christianity. They want to return to their *pon-hyang* and live together eternally in heaven and rise again with Jesus Christ.

Faith in heaven gives Korean American Christians hope and courage to live even when they are faced with hardship. Faith breathes life into them. Being certain of where we will go after death is very assuring. We also understand that God alone is in charge of our life and death and that this understanding helps us to accept death when it comes because it happens at God's chosen time. In fact, one may even hear someone say to those who are lamenting over the death of their loved one, "Please stop weeping. Don't you know that s/he is now in a better place in heaven where there is no more weeping and sickness?" Nevertheless, death is a hostile human condition, and many Korean American Christians take death as a punishment of one's sins, especially when death happens suddenly, unexpectedly, or after a long illness. One of the authors heard the following:

> My grandpa was revered as a pious man by his church members throughout his life. He fell ill in his fifties; however, right after the Korean War half of his body became paralyzed. To make it worse, he had lost everything during the war and his family was left dirt poor. He never recovered health and died several years later. My mom said that, observing this, some church members remarked, "Elder Noh must have done something really bad in his life that we don't know about. Otherwise, how could he have suffered so much and die?"

Here we see the speaker speculating the merit of Elder Noh's life. In her view, he did not die well. The speaker's question may have been prompted by the contradiction the speaker must have experienced in Elder Noh's death, especially if she believed in the logic of cause and effect and a direct connection between living well and dying well. This kind of reasoning is problematic when we consider that the world in which we live is an imperfect world in which so many innocent people suffer from many injustices, even death, and no one, even the most virtuous, is immune from diseases, accidents, and human and natural tragedies that take away life. As a people of faith, we must be careful not to give into human speculations when we are dealing with mysteries such as death. These matters belong to God.

Death is an inevitable human condition that is shared by everyone, regardless of class, gender, and race. The Korean American church continues to give its faith community the hope of eternal life in heaven and provide opportunities of healing in times of death. By participating in practices of prayer, mourning, and caring, we become agents of healing for one another, beyond the circle of biological family. How is the Korean American Christian church then dealing with the reality of death of those who are outside the circle of its faith community, those who are considered to be "nonbelievers"? One response may be for all in the Korean American church to throw themselves into evangelistic efforts to save the nonbelievers from an eternal life in hell. This response is indeed witnessed among many Korean American Christians, young and old, who go on mission trips throughout the world, with a goal of making converts out of those who do not believe in Jesus. Some zealous evangelists say that this effort must continue even if conversion may mean severe persecution and death to the newly converted.

The message of heaven does give hope to those who are suffering, and many turn to Christ, hoping for a better life beyond death. It helps them die well. But we must not forget that Jesus taught his disciples to pray for heaven on earth. It is a plea that God's will be done on earth as it is in heaven. In this regard, caution must be exercised in turning the idea of heaven into a metaphysical concept out of touch with life on earth. We need to ask whether this message of heaven has not made the faith perspective of Korean American Christians too disengaged and only concerned with what happens after death. What about the human conditions that kill people, such as economic exploitation, racism, violence, homophobia, ecological crisis, and war? What is our response as a faith community to this kind of dying?

Practices such as holding a memorial service for those who have passed on indeed help the practitioners appreciate the life circle that continues on through human connections and through generations. It helps the practitioners of faith live well on a day-to-day basis, and it prepares us to die well. Jesus said, "I came that they may have life, and have it abundantly" (John 10:10b). In order for the practices of faith by Korean American Christians to be life-giving to others, our faith community must commit itself to develop practices of faith that truly resource the life circle that includes everyone here and now. This practice of resourcing the life circle challenges us to reach out to those who are not dying well and those who are experiencing cruel death-dealing forces that destroy life.

QUESTIONS FOR REFLECTION

1. What are some of your experiences of dealing with death? What practices have helped you deal with these experiences of death? How have they informed your life?
2. In the traditional Korean context, death is not necessarily experienced as an end of life. Therefore, the indigenous practice of dying well in the Korean context is integrated into the practice of living well, which resources the life circle. What is your understanding of death and dying? What does the Bible teach us about death and dying? In what ways do you see Korean American practices of dying well becoming incorporated into mainstream America's practice of dealing with death?
3. Discuss the relationship between the Christian notion of forgiveness and the Korean American practice of forgiving the dead.

4. Different cultures and faith traditions have different practices of dying well. Mexicans, for example, observe *Dia de Los Muertos* (the Day of the Dead), which runs for two days. The first day is to honor children who have died, and the second day is to honor deceased adults. The tradition is largely to remember the dead ones who Mexicans believe will come and visit the living. The main observance of the day is to dine on the special holiday bread and share the feast with the dead. For Roman Catholics, remembering the dead on the Feast of All Souls (Nov. 2) and praying for them is a common practice. One way to engage in this practice is by remembering on Feast Days the saints of the church who have died, leaving the church community with a model of a holy life. Another way to engage in this practice is to remember the dead by offering intercessory prayers for the purification of the souls of the loved ones in purgatory.[13] These prayers may be spontaneous prayers reaching out to loved ones, or more formal praying, or a mass of remembrance. Drawing on the discussion of the Korean American practice of dying well, compare the Korean American practice with the above two examples. What lessons can we learn from these practices of dying well?

Chapter 6

Bearing Wisdom

The Practice of Shaping the Generations Ahead

> *She has just graduated from high school. Her father, who is in Korea and cannot attend the graduation ceremony, wants to express his heartfelt love for her. He seeks out a calligraphy artist friend and asks him to write, "Faith, Hope, and Love" in Chinese characters. When he comes back to her in the United States, he is holding a large framed calligraphy artwork to be given to her daughter as a graduation gift.*
>
> —from a story retold by Unzu

Koreans have long recognized that wisdom is a valuable resource for one's self-realization and in the shaping of a community. Traditionally, people have given as gifts to each other words of wisdom that enlighten the mind and strengthen the heart. These words are written on paper or cloth in refined calligraphy. Often nicely framed or presented in the form of hanging scrolls, they decorate the walls of the spaces inhabited by Korean Americans. They are fine artworks that clearly increase the aesthetic quality of living, but they are certainly much more than decorative. They are written teachings for everyone to see, read, and learn the wisdom.

WRITING WISDOM ON THE WALLS

> *He who knows these three things [wisdom, honesty, and courage] knows how to cultivate his personal life. Knowing how to govern his personal life, he knows how to govern other men. And knowing how to govern other men, he knows how to govern the empire, its states, and the families.*
>
> (*Chung-yung* xx:11)[1]

> *The fear of the Lord is the beginning of knowledge;*
> *fools despise wisdom and instruction.*
>
> (Prov. 1:7)

It is a common practice for a Korean family to have *ka-hoon* (family precepts) framed and hung high at a prominent place for all members of the family to see. *Ka-hoon* is proverbial, and it guides the family's life. Probably a practice originated in the literati class, it is something that is now commonly practiced by a variety of human institutions, including the church. In many of the spaces inhabited by people like the home, school, business, and church, one can see value-laden proverbial verses displayed in prominent places. These words are not the rules to live by. Rather, they are precepts that are supposed to serve as a guide to lead people in the right path of life. They are the words of wisdom of the old that teach the young how to live their lives.

These written teachings come in a variety of forms, including poetry, proverbial sayings, or excerpts from classical Confucian texts. Some examples are "Don't try to win the world, but give it what you can" or "Do not take the road unless it is the Way." They can be just a few Chinese characters imbued with lots of significant meaning, such as *sung-sil* (誠實)(genuineness and sincerity) and *sang-ho jon-jung* (相互尊重)(mutual respect). Since these texts are chosen by the elders in the family, they also carry a lot of authority.

In recent years, many of the verses used in Korean American Christian homes and other institutions have become scriptural, often from Proverbs but from other parts of the Bible as well. Some are direct quotes, and others are adaptations of the scriptural text. "The fear of the Lord is the beginning of knowledge; fools despise wisdom and instruction (Prov. 1:7)" is one favorite verse appearing often in homes. "*Kyung Chun Ae In* [敬天愛人]," which means "Fear God and Love Neighbor," a set of four Chinese characters featured in many homes, is an adaptation of a biblical teaching. The Beatitudes in Matthew 5, 1 Corinthians 13, Philippians 4:4–7, and Psalm 23 and other psalms that praise the greatness of God are some of the favorite texts that Koreans write on scrolls in their entirety in calligraphy as a gift to the people they love and care about.

Church communities also engage in the same practice. A verse that is often in churches is "You shall be holy, for I the LORD your God am holy" (Lev. 19:2b). Other scriptural texts that are frequently seen include the following:

"The righteous live by their faith." (Hab. 2:4b)

"'Come to me, all you that are weary and are carrying heavy burdens, and I will give you rest.'" (Matt. 11:28)

"'Do not let your hearts be troubled. Believe in God, believe also in me.'" (John 14:1)

"I can do all things through him who strengthens me." (Phil. 4:13a)

"I will make of you a great nation, and I will bless you, and make your name great, so that you will be a blessing." (Gen. 12:2)

"'For mortals it is impossible, but for God all things are possible.'" (Matt. 19:26b)

Many of these texts remind the readers of God's presence and power and guide their faithful living.

One verse that is often displayed in Korean business settings speaks of God's promise. It says, "Though your beginning was small, your latter days will be very great" (Job 8:7). Korean Americans of various religious backgrounds who enter these spaces do not seem to mind such practice because regardless of the source, they are there to impart wisdom rather than impose one's religion on others. This practice reminds us of the words of God given to Israel as Hebrews were about to start their new life in the land of Canaan:

> Hear, O Israel: The LORD is our God, the LORD alone. You shall love the LORD your God with all your heart, and with all your soul, and with all your might. Keep these words that I am commanding you today in your heart. Recite them to your children and talk about them when you are at home and when you are away, when you lie down and when you rise. Bind them as a sign on your hand, fix them as an emblem on your forehead, and write them on the doorposts of your house and on your gates. (Deut. 6:4–5).

Korean American Christians have definitely heard these words and heeded the command.

MY HEART DESIRES THE WISDOM OF THE LORD

> The law of the LORD is perfect,
>   reviving the soul;
> the decrees of the LORD are sure,
>   making wise the simple;
> the precepts of the LORD are right,
>   rejoicing the heart;
> . . . .
> More to be desired are they than gold,
>   even much fine gold;
> sweeter also than honey,
>   and drippings of the honeycomb.
>   (Ps. 19:7–8a, 10)

A family gathers in a circle for a time of family worship. After a prayer and hymn singing, everyone opens one's own Bible. The head of the family who leads the worship begins reading a passage from where the family left off the day before. The family members go around the circle reading a paragraph each until the circle is completed. Following the Scripture reading, they end with a prayer. This type of Scripture reading in the Korean American family context begins from Genesis and continues on until they are finished with reading the last verse in the Revelation to John. When they are done with reading the entire Bible, they begin reading from Genesis again, and this process goes on continuously. Each beginning and ending is dated. Although Korean American Christians regard the Bible study an integral part of their spiritual life, this type of Scripture reading is also an extremely important practice for Korean American Christians. It matters to have read the entire Bible, not once or twice, but many times throughout one's lifetime.

Perhaps this practice is connected to the way Koreans have traditionally led their devotional life. Korean women, in particular, are well known for their deep spirituality, practiced through daily rituals. Most women in the past were in charge of their own spiritual lives, and they practiced their faith by prayerfully offering a bowl of clear water to the Spirit at early dawn every day. Trusting that sincerity moves the heavens, women would pour out their sincere hearts of desire to the Spirit. Although most were illiterate, some of them would recite every day the Buddhist mantra with rosary. For those who could read, men in particular, they practiced their spirituality by reading the Confucian and/or Buddhist texts on a daily basis.

With conversion to Christianity in the Korean context, the illiterate converts learned to read and write in order to read the Bible and sing hymns. This practice was most evident among women. Most women were illiterate, but a majority who could read could do so only in *Han-gul* (Korean written language) and not so much in *Han-moon* (Chinese written language), the written language of the male literati class. Interestingly, the Bible that was introduced to Koreans was written in Korean, making it easily accessible to women and the lower class, which made up the majority of the population. As they used to draw near to the Spirit every morning by offering a bowl of water, women individually drew near to the Scripture, which was understood as the embodiment of God's wisdom. They read it, memorized the verses, and wrote them in their hearts. When the entire family had converted, Scripture reading became a family ritual practiced on a daily basis; this time, however, the reading was usually led by the patriarch of the family.

The Scripture that enlightens the mind with its wisdom has accompanied Korean and Korean American Christians on a daily basis. Even today, Scripture reading and memorizing continue to play a vital role in one's faithful living. The practice of reading and memorizing is rigorously followed, and the church reinforces the practice in a variety of ways, including contests. It is the wisdom and power they seek through the practice, for it is written that the word of the Lord enlightens the eyes and makes the simple wise. In a world that is torn in so many ways with conflicting virtues and teachings, the wisdom of the Lord found in the Scripture leads the practitioners of faith to still waters and empowers them to live more confidently with the knowledge that God is with them.

This practice, however, has its dangers as well. So strictly followed, it can make the practitioner rigid and unreflective. Such a practice may turn the Scripture into a code book of dos and don'ts. Thus, rather than forming people to use their God-given abilities to intuit, to read the signs around them, to listen to one another compassionately, and to learn from human endeavors such as science that search for truth, this practice has the potential to make people narrow-minded, fearful, and legalistic. Instead of letting God's wisdom transform them into wise persons with a big, forgiving, and embracing heart and a mind open to new insights and revelations, such skewed practice may have turned some of them into poor students of God's infinite wisdom, which surpasses human understanding. It would be helpful to teach Korean American practitioners of Christian faith a variety of ways to encounter the Scripture so that the Spirit of God may teach us the depth, breadth, and width of God's infinite wisdom revealed in human imperfect language.

WISDOM AND HONOR

Happy are those who find wisdom,
 and those who get understanding,
for her income is better than silver,
 and her revenue better than gold.
She is more precious than jewels,
 and nothing you desire can compare with her.
Long life is in her right hand;
 in her left hand are riches and honor.
(Prov. 3:13–16)

Often, older Korean Americans would say, "Wisdom of the old is never wrong [*Yet-mal teul-in-gut ha-na-do up-da*]" in the middle of a conversation before inserting a very appropriate old saying to make his or her point. In that moment, the age-old truth that never fades erases the temporal gap and shines its face again. Those of us living in the present resonate with the wisdom passed on to us by those from ages ago. Inherent in this understanding is that life itself is the best teacher. It is an understanding that time is cyclical rather than linear and that history repeats itself. Korean children grow up being nurtured by such wisdom of the old. These wise sayings shape the emerging generation's perspective on life, relations, and the world. Respect for the old among Korean Americans is then a natural outcome, expressed in a variety of ways. For instance, elders of a church community often have a separate table of honor prepared for them during the time of fellowship. Some churches would even have the young children practice a Korean bowing ritual to all of the church elders on a special holiday, such as the Lunar New Year's Day, hoping that the rites would teach children to respect and honor the elders.

One way Korean Americans honor their older adults is by bestowing upon them leadership status. This practice has its root in the Confucian tradition that understood politics "as a process of rectification" and the art of government as "an extension of moral education."[2] In this tradition, a sage, a wise man, was considered to be most fit to serve as king. It is then no wonder that many Korean American church communities across the denominational lines have adopted the Presbyterian system of electing "elders" for lay leadership.[3] Even the term "elder" itself is appropriate to the Korean American context since it is culturally assumed that wisdom comes with aging. One woman recounts her experience:

> I have been a lifetime Presbyterian, but I had no idea what becoming an elder meant for the first generation until my father became an elder. He became an elder when I was doing a year of study in Korea. One day before his ordination, I received a package of invitations to be sent out to his friends in Korea. That gave me a hint that elder ordination meant much more than what I thought. Later on I heard that my family threw a huge party for the church and the guests with lots of food in celebration of this honor on his ordination day. For someone like me who thinks of the office of elder primarily as a seat of governance, this experience with my father's ordination felt somewhat strange, but to my mother's and grandmother's generation, this was a big event not only for my father but for the entire family. This experience made me realize that elder ordination meant much more than becoming a member of the governing session in a church. It meant being granted a highest status of honor in a community.—from a story retold by Unzu

In such a community, older adults are almost always the only ones chosen as "elders" for leadership, and younger Korean Americans grow up thinking that leadership only belongs to the old. Those who think of church governance in terms of representative politics have a hard time understanding this. It makes sense only when we consider how we, consciously or unconsciously, value wisdom that comes from life experiences. This honoring system is, however, highly gendered because it is only older male adults who are almost invariably chosen as "elders." Even though a few older women have started to enter the ranks of elders in recent years in Korean American churches of certain mainline denominations that ordain women as elders, the office is still predominantly male in membership. This reflects the Korean/Korean American situation that often interprets any type of difference into role difference. Although respect for elders cuts across the gender line in the highly gendered and hierarchical Korean familial context, the highest decision-making authority is almost always conferred to male elders. Still, this respect for elders is probably what motivated the Korean Presbyterian church leadership to create a position of *Kwon-sa* for older women of faith. Any mature woman of faith who has served as a deacon and has come of mature age almost always becomes a *Kwon-sa*.[4]

The office of *Kwon-sa* is a position of high honor for women in the Korean American churches that have incorporated the Korean Presbyterian system that grew out of the Korean context. *Kwon-sas* are the spiritual pillars of the church, although they are not members of the decision-making body. They are the praying women. They often serve as regular companions of male ministers when the ministers make house visitations, especially when they are visiting a female parishioner. In times of seeking discernment, even authoritarian male ministers often turn to these women for words of wisdom that comes from their intense prayer life and years of life experiences. Often, these women know what male elders do not. They are informal advisors to ministers and many times to their husbands who are elders of the church. Since they are outside the power structure, they may appear to be no threat to ministers and elders. However, although their influence is only indirect structurally, *Kwon-sas* are more likely than others to have very direct and intimate influence on the ministers and elders on a personal level. Moreover, they may together become a powerful group with a large influence.

DOES NOT GOD ALSO GIVE US WISDOM?

*"'Out of the mouths of infants and nursing babies
you have prepared praise for yourself.'"*
(Matt. 21:16b)

Wisdom is indeed a valuable resource for a community, and the people of wisdom deserve respect and honor. The other side of this practice is that the old feel a genuine responsibility to nurture the young with their wisdom. This manifests itself very well in Korean American churches where one can find many young college-aged adults serving as Sunday school teachers to their younger brothers and sisters. In this regard, this practice is a good critique on the current trend in Western culture that is causing pain between generations due to the devaluation of aging. In the Korean American context, the practice of honoring the old for their wisdom is an invaluable inheritance.

Granted, the idea of governance in the Confucian context is very different from that of the West based on the political philosophy of Aristotelian democracy.[5] However, when we consider that our faith is practiced in North America, where politics of diversity has historically been a key to the shifting dynamics of social organization, one wonders if honoring must always happen in the form of ordination to a position of power in the governing body, especially when we consider that the church community is made up of diverse groups of people. As previously discussed, the practice of ordination in the Korean American context is largely gender biased and age biased. It is difficult to refute the argument coming from emerging generations that this honoring system discriminates against the young—a reverse form of ageism that exists in the mainstream U.S. culture. The same is true of the gender bias. Younger women of the emerging generations, who no longer experience sexism to the degree that their elders experienced in the past, have difficulty being part of the community that discriminates against them because they are female. When one considers the silent exodus of emerging generations from the Korean American faith communities, this is a serious issue that should raise concern. After all, Jesus praised the wisdom of the young by saying, "'I thank you, Father, Lord of heaven and earth, because you have hidden these things from the wise and the intelligent and have revealed them to infants'" (Matt. 11:25).

Several questions can be raised on this issue. Doesn't the current practice limit the vitality of the Spirit that has been promised to all flesh (Acts 2:17)? Doesn't this practice of limiting leadership to male elders somehow give them permission to have unlimited power without any possibility for check and balance? What can a community do when elders who sit in positions of power abuse their authority instead of imparting wisdom? What can and should be done when the elders misguide their community by abusing their power? How can they be held accountable? How can the integrity of the faith community be saved from this reverse ageism and sexism? Is this practice justifiable in the name of culture? What kind of alternative structure can we create that would allow the Korean American faith community to give recognition to the wisdom of elders while giving full and equal access to everyone in the faith community to positions of leadership?

The gospel of Jesus has touched hundreds and thousands of the hearts of the oppressed with its liberating power, empowering them to become "somebody" when the world treated them as "nobody." Women and children who have been historically treated as nobodies in the patriarchal family and society cannot help but challenge this practice. If life itself is the best teacher for wisdom, many women who have been through the hills, valleys, and deserts certainly should have much more wisdom than privileged men to impart and guide the church community. As the emerging generations in the Korean American context are coming of age, they are beginning to change this practice, and some changes are taking place even in the first-generation context, slowly but surely. They are asking, Doesn't God also give us wisdom?

QUESTIONS FOR REFLECTION

1. Can you identify some family precepts you grew up with? Do you still live by them?
2. The passages that appear below are often found in the Korean American Christian homes and businesses. What kind of wisdom do these verses impart?

"The LORD is my shepherd, I shall not want.
    He makes me lie down in green pastures;
he leads me beside still waters." (Ps. 23:1, 2)

"'Do not let your hearts be troubled. Believe in God, believe also in me.'" (John 14:1)

"Though your beginning was small,
    your latter days will be very great." (Job 8:7)

"So let us not grow weary in doing what is right, for we will reap at harvest time, if we do not give up." (Gal. 6:9)

"If I speak in the tongues of mortals and of angels, but do not have love, I am a noisy gong or a clanging cymbal." (1 Cor. 13:1)

3. What are some of the ways you approach the Scripture to gain wisdom? What kind of practices go with your Scripture reading?
4. In the Korean American context, the practice of honoring often goes hand in hand with power. For instance, not all wise people are honored equally: male and female, old and young. What are some ways by which the Korean American Christian community can honor the wisdom of those who are not recognized?
5. Wisdom is an important resource in the Korean American community. How does mainstream America value wisdom as an important source of shaping a community? How does the way you perceive wisdom influence the way you treat the elderly?

Chapter 7

Gathering at the Well

The Practice of Building Community

So Isaac departed from there and camped in the valley of Gerar and settled there. Isaac dug again the wells of water that had been dug in the days of his father Abraham; for the Philistines had stopped them up after the death of Abraham; and he gave them the names that his father had given them. But when Isaac's servants dug in the valley and found there a well of spring water, the herders of Gerar quarreled with Isaac's herders, saying, "The water is ours." So he called the well Esek, because they contended with him. Then they dug another well, and they quarreled over that one also; so he called it Sitnah. He moved from there and dug another well, and they did not quarrel over it; so he called it Rehoboth, saying, "Now the LORD has made room for us, and we shall be fruitful in the land."

(Gen. 26:17–22)

So [Jesus] came to a Samaritan city called Sychar, near the plot of ground that Jacob had given to his son Joseph. Jacob's well was there, and Jesus, tired out by his journey, was sitting by the well. It was about noon.

A Samaritan woman came to draw water, and Jesus said to her, "Give me a drink."... The Samaritan woman said to him, "How is it that you, a Jew, ask a drink of me, a woman of Samaria?"... Jesus answered her, "If you knew the gift of God, and who it is that is saying to you, 'Give me a drink,' you would have asked him, and he would have given you living water." The woman said to him, "Sir, you have no bucket, and the well is deep. Where do you get that living water? Are you greater than our ancestor Jacob, who gave us the well, and with his sons and his flocks drank from it?"

(John 4:5–12)

COMMUNITY AT THE WELL

A well, a source of water, in the traditional communities was an important center for the life of a community. Even in contemporary societies, a well continues to serve the same vital function in many parts of the world. Particularly in a dry climate, water has long been a dire necessity for survival. Because of this important survival function, the well becomes a center of community. First, a well is a natural gathering place for the sustenance and essential nourishment that are life-giving. Second, a well is a place where people gather to socialize; to share events of the day, the happenings of the village, or gossip; or to take part in other social transactions important to the community. It becomes a center for the re-membering of community.

In Genesis, Isaac is sandwiched between his father Abraham and his son Jacob. He has little active agency in the history of the Israelites. His claim to fame is the obedience shown in the face of his own sacrifice by his father Abraham. He is given a wife and he has sons, one of whom tricks him. It seems from the story that the only active agency he exercises is in the practice of digging wells. An important legacy he leaves his descendants is the wells he dug. Digging wells might well be thought of as his vocation.[1]

Like Isaac's digging wells in many locations, Korean American Protestant Christians have dug many wells in the form of founding churches. As the saying goes, "When Chinese come to the United States, they start restaurants; when Japanese come to the United States, they start businesses; when Koreans come to the United States, they start churches." With the founding of churches, Korean Americans create many important structures for the survival of themselves as a people and a community:

- Social services that help negotiate changes in immigration status and that teach basic survival skills, such as the English language.
- Social support networks that help create friendships, a sense of belonging, and a means of mentoring each other through family struggles.
- Church programs that help develop and support a deep, abiding faith within the community.
- Various other modalities through which cultural identity formation is celebrated and supported, such as Korean language school, church family meals in which Korean food is celebrated and served to young and old, and youth programs and parenting classes through which Korean American Christians can engage positively in discussions about the tension between assimilation and cultural preservation.

Although these structures function to help the survival of immigrants, they also promote the health and well-being of the Korean American community. Like water and wells in traditional communities, churches help not only with the survival of the Korean American community but with the ongoing health of its communal relationships. Thus digging wells in the form of building churches is an important practice.

The practice of creating churches also forms community. For Korean immigrant Christians living in the United States, the process of community formation is one that is negotiated through many factors, such as tradition, history, lifestyle, theology, social and structural discriminations, generational differences, and personal affinities. Given this context, the story of the woman at the well can be read in a fresh perspective. Most often, commentators and preachers focus on the undesirableness of this Samaritan woman's social standing and her reputation for having multiple partners. She comes to draw water in the heat of the day to avoid meeting other people who might cast judgment on her lifestyle. This marginalized woman is given a chance at receiving the "living water," and she takes it while other righteous religious people cannot hear the good news.

However, what is perhaps more interesting from the Korean American perspective is her question to Jesus, "Are you greater than our ancestor Jacob, who gave us the well, and with his sons and his flocks drank from it?" (John 4:12). This question is one that is pertinent to Korean Americans struggling to negotiate the competing influences of the indigenous religions and the overlay of Christian conservative theology given by missionaries. Does the Samaritan woman need to abandon the well of her ancestor, Jacob, in order to receive the "living water"? Or, having received the "living water," can she then go and draw water from her ancestor's well without shame? Similarly, Korean Americans must ask themselves, Can we draw from the ancestor's wells of shamanic, Confucian, Buddhist, and Taoist roots and still be faithful Christians? Or, must we abandon the wells of our ancestors in order to receive the "living water"?[2]

In this struggle of negotiating between what to keep and what to throw out, we form community. This negotiation occurs in many forms: religious, cultural, generational, and linguistic. The practice of community formation requires members to tease out what is the "normative" and "acceptable" core of what a community believes. When conflict occurs in this negotiation or when negotiation does not happen at all, very often the community splits as a way to relieve the tension. This points to the schismatic tendencies of Korean American churches in general.[3] Social scientists and others have noticed the explosive growth of Korean American churches, which stems partly from the splitting of existing churches as well as the creation of new ones. When a new community is formed through splitting, it carries with it the traumas caused by the schism.

COMMUNITY OF HEALING

For the Korean American community to survive this dynamic, it must understand the need for healing in the community and the practices that deliver this healing. Thus, any discussion of community formation necessarily includes a discussion of healing. Healing understood as re-membering into a community gives one a broader perspective than focusing solely on a deliverance from physical and mental illness in a person. Very often, Korean American Christians spiritualize illness and recognize the need for spiritual wellness before they can be healed from the physical and the mental. The following vignette illustrates the faith healing that is a common practice in which Korean Americans engage to seek deliverance from sickness.

> It was very crowded. Everyone was animated with air of expectation. This faith healer had a reputation of being really good. People gathered from all over the city to witness and to be healed. The service started with singing and then moved on to preaching. The gathered people had to be ready spiritually to accept healing. So the faith healing preacher kept preaching until he thought the congregation was ready and the Spirit was filling the place. Then he asked his helpers to assist him as people went up for *an-su ki-do* ("laying on of hands"). He placed his hand on each one's forehead and shouted, "In the name of Jesus, be healed." The recipients, then, started to fall backwards where the attendants waited to catch them as they fell. They were then assisted as they got up and went back to their seats. Certain people had visible sicknesses, like a back problem or walking with a cane. But others had problems or issues they wanted discernment on. The preacher would call out, "Is there someone here who is struggling with chest pains?" or "Is there someone here who is worried about a decision that needs to be made?" The congregation watched and prayed to assist the healer. And towards the end of the healing service, he would call anyone who would like to receive a blessing.—from an experience of healing service retold by Su Yon

The congregants in the vignette hold onto a promise of healing. They know that the gospel is inundated with stories about Jesus' ministry that repeatedly showed the power of healing. They remember Jesus' words, "Your faith has made you well." Their faith in healing is also rooted in their identification of their savior as the wounded healer who, by his suffering, takes away their sickness, as understood by the prophet Isaiah:

> Surely he has borne our griefs
>   and carried our sorrows;
> yet we esteemed him stricken,
>   smitten by God, and afflicted.
> But he was wounded for our transgressions,
>   he was bruised for our iniquities;
> upon him was the chastisement that made us whole,
>   and with his stripes we are healed.
>   (Isa. 53:4–5 RSV)

This Isaiah passage is one of the most often-cited ones during worship services, prayer meetings, and healing services. This is no surprise given that as a historically oppressed people living in the United States, the cry for healing characterizes the faith of Korean American Christians. The majority of the Korean American community live with many wounds inflicted on them through devastating historical events. Moreover, many Korean immigrants in the United States live with a sense of estrangement, status loss, and anomaly, all of which cause dramatic loss of meaning and brokenness within each individual and the community as a whole.

This experience of painful suffering for the Korean American people is called *han*, a Korean word to describe the depth of human suffering. *Han* is defined as "a sense of unresolved resentment against injustice suffered; a sense of helplessness because of the overwhelming odds against one's self; a feeling of acute pain or sorrows; and an obstinate urge to take 'revenge' and to right the wrong."[4] *Han* is not just an individual reality; it is also a collective reality. *Han*, brokenness in human reality, has to do with dis-ease that is caused when right relations are broken. Thus healing takes on a different significance. Healing has to do with realigning the broken relations so that right relations are recovered between oneself and the other, the living and the dead, oneself and the spirit(s), and so on. Healing is therefore an act of re-membering the community.

Koreans have traditionally sought to resolve or to untangle *han* through indigenous religious practices like *mu-sok* (shamanic practices). Through *kut* (shamanistic ritual), which was often a community or village event, the diseased (both the living and dead) received healing and were re-membered as a community.[5] In Korean shamanism, the cause of the illness of a person is seen as having not merely an individual but also a communal source. Therefore, healing must address not only the individual's sickness but also the sickness in the relationships of the wider family circle. Allowing the family members to vent their frustrations in the name of the gods, distorted family interactions are healed. They are then reconciled to each other through the mediation of powerful and benevolent ancestors.[6]

However, one of the unfortunate legacies of the "Christianized Korea" is the forced abandonment of the indigenous religious practices that were communal in nature and at the core and root of Koreans as a people.[7] When Protestant missionaries came to Korea over one hundred years ago, they imposed Western Protestant Christian practices (particular ways to worship, pray, and sing, for instance) over and against indigenous Korean practices. As Korean people converted to Christianity, they converted from their indigenous religious and cultural practices to Western Protestant Christian practices. Rituals such as *kut* were forbidden since they were seen as idolatrous and evil. As Korean theologian David Kwang-sun Suh writes, "Early mission success stories featured the new converts burning all of the house spirits of the *mu-dang* [shaman] religion."[8] Although these communal indigenous practices were suppressed, they remained rooted deep in the Korean psyche.

Thus, on the surface, Korean Christians converted from shamanism and other religions to Western Christianity. However, in effect, the indigenous practices were so integrated into the Korean worldview that they influenced the development of Korean Christianity, creating shamanized Christian practices. Some scholars argue that perhaps it is that very shamanistic mind-set of the Korean people that created a fertile ground for receiving Christianity. In a way, Christianity fulfilled a similar role for Korean people as shamanistic practice had. It is quite possible that Jesus was understood by early Korean Christians steeped in shamanism as the shaman (*mu-dang*) par excellence who healed the sick and cast out demons. So, although the outward shaman ritual practices were not allowed, the internal elements of the shamanistic ritual (*kut*) were carried over by Christian practices. Christian practices are laden with shamanistic meanings and equivalences—for example, the healing ritual of *an-su ki-do*, a practice discussed in the earlier discussion of fervent prayer. Before a *mu-dang* can begin to heal, she must be possessed by a spirit and reach a state of ecstasy through singing and dancing. Similarly, in a Korean healing ritual of *an-su ki-do*, possession by the Holy Spirit is an important element. With the power of the Holy Spirit, a Christian healer can speak in tongues, chase out demons, and cure the sick.

In fact, the purpose of many of the revival meetings of Korean American Christians is to be filled with the Holy Spirit (*sung-ryung choong-man*). By highlighting the Pentecost story and the acts of the early Christians who were deemed always to be filled with the Holy Spirit, these revival meetings emphasize the necessity of living everyday life filled with the Spirit. The words of Paul echo the experience of their existence in the United States: "And now, as a captive to the Spirit, I am on my way to Jerusalem, not knowing what will happen to me there, except that the Holy Spirit testifies to me in every city that imprisonment and persecutions are waiting for me" (Acts 20:22–23). The Holy Spirit plays a dual role, both as an agent who "testifies to them" of their persecutions and as the one that empowers them to deal with the "persecutions" of everyday life.

The act of being filled with the Spirit in order for healing to happen is usually focused on an individual. The Christianized form of shamanistic healing has lost some of its important communal function. In *kut*, healing comes about by realigning the break or the dis-ease in the family/community relationships. Unfortunately, a particular Protestant worldview that was imposed on the early Christians in Korea was very individualistic in nature. Uncritically absorbed by people, it served to disconnect the Christian sense of healing from the people's communal roots of the shamanistic practice. Thus, the practice of healing in Korean American churches is predominantly individualistic in nature.

The result of this tendency is that community formation, which demands both individual and communal healing to be effective, is truncated. Since it is limited to the individual, Christian healing as commonly practiced cannot function to heal the community as an entire entity. When healing is focused on individuals rather than the community, individual needs and ideological standpoints become paramount, rather than community cohesion. In this context, individual needs are often met through schism. Rather than seeking consensus around conflicting ideological points of view or differing leadership styles, Korean American churches tend to split into their own like-minded groups. On the one hand, this allows them to keep their principles and to maintain the integrity of their stance. On the other hand, it places lesser value on the unity of a larger group.

The effect of this, however negative it may seem, is to create a fertile ground for church growth and evangelism. Like Isaac and the dispute over the ownership of wells, which prompted Isaac to go and dig other wells, Korean American churches' growth is fueled by this dynamic of forming–breaking–reforming. Furthermore, this dynamic achieves several things in the process. It creates space to transgress boundaries of mainline Korean American Protestant religion, and it allows for "experimental" churches to flourish across the ideological spectrum. From house churches to churches for college students to churches for wives of the U.S. military servicemen, new churches are constantly being created to meet the needs of specific groups.

COMMUNITY OF RE-MEMBERING

Well-digging is impossible to do alone. It is a labor-intensive task that takes a community of people working together. But once a well is dug, it becomes a source of life, health, and well-being, vital for the survival of the community. In the same manner, the practice of community formation is also a communal and labor-intensive task. Often born out of conflict, it can be a practice that makes diversity thrive. However, it is important to consider what is let go of and what is held onto in that process. Like the Samaritan woman at the well, the tension between the practices of the ancestors and the new practices presents itself when forming community. Korean American churches have done well, perhaps too well, in honoring and preserving the new practices of the Christian missionaries. It is time to reflect on what indigenous roots Koreans/Korean American Christians have let go of in this process. Healing is an example. They have successfully incorporated the individualistic element of traditional healing practices into their version of Christian practices but have lost the communal element. Individual healing practices need to be replaced and rediscovered within the healing context of the community. In this way, attending to communal responsibility becomes a form of healing, both for the individual and for the group. Embracing the communal aspect of Korean American practices enhances the re-membering of a people into communities. The digging of new wells, as well as the letting go of wells, is perhaps a vocational vision for Korean American Protestants.

QUESTIONS FOR REFLECTION

1. What are some of the ancestral wells from which you draw water? How do your ancestral wells sustain you? How does the living water you draw from the church sustain you? Are there any conflicts between your ancestral wells and the church's claim of needing only the "living water"?

2. To sustain their community, Korean Americans have dug other wells besides church, such as the community center and battered women's shelter. What other forms of well-digging can you identify for Korean American Christians?

3. There are two images evoked when seeking healing: the all-powerful, all-present God and the wounded healer embodied in Jesus. Which images would you evoke when seeking healing?

4. Have you experienced schism in your church life? If so, what would you have done to prevent it and why?

5. When Isaac's well was contested, he always gave in and went on to dig another. Instead of digging a separate well, could he have negotiated with other communities to share the same well? For instance, do racially/ethnically specified communities need separate wells? Are there other alternative models of building communities?

Chapter 8

Thy Will Be Done

The Practice of Piety

> *Let me have no shame*
> *Under the heaven*
> *Till I die.*
> *Even winds among the foliage*
> *Pained my heart.*
>
> *With a heart that sings of the stars,*
> *I'll love all dying things.*
> *And I must fare the path*
> *That's been allotted to me.*
>
> *Tonight also the winds sweep over the stars.*[1]
> —by Yun Dong-Ju

PIETISTIC LIVING (*KYUNG-GUN-HAN SAENG-WHAL*)

The Korean tradition historically puts much emphasis on self-cultivation. Pietistic practices were considered essential for becoming fully human. Korean children were taught from an early age to cultivate/shine/polish their mind-heart (*ma-eum*) diligently every day to become a good person so that they would not have shame under heaven. Upholding self-cultivation as the goal of education, families and schools all tried to teach important human character attributes or moral precepts that they felt were most important for educating the young to become fully human according to Confucian understanding. Whatever the choice of precepts or attributes may be, they were usually highly personal and relational concepts that focused on cultivating self and promoting balance and harmony.

75

In the Confucian worldview, where self is the center of the universe, what one does with oneself can affect the lives of others, including the whole universe. In other words, there is cosmic significance to how a person lives out his or her life. In this worldview, heaven, the originator of all things, including humans, has an operating principle (*do* [道], meaning "way") that keeps everything in perfect order and harmony. Inherent in everything created under heaven is also a unique principle (*li* [理]) that is true to its nature. When one realizes one's *li*, she or he would have unfolded the heaven-endowed nature. By so doing, one would have followed the Way (*do*) and contributed to the order and harmony of the cosmos. In this scheme of things, following one's own selfish desires against the heavenly principle that orders the cosmos is evil, a cardinal sin.

Since the locus of self is understood to be *ma-eum*, one's attainment of goodness depends on cultivating one's mind-heart in order that it can best reflect the heavenly principle like a clean mirror would. For Yi T'oegye, an accomplished sixteenth-century Korean scholar in neo-Confucian thought, self-cultivation involved "blocking human desires and preserving Heavenly principle" in order that one's mind-heart can identify with the principle of heaven.[2] In sum, the goal of self-cultivation for Yi T'oegye was to achieve unity between one's mind-heart and the Way of Heaven, and he saw piety as key to self-cultivation. The goal of self-cultivation meant becoming a sage, a moral perfection, therefore, fully human.

One Korean scholar has argued that this concept of self-cultivation parallels the concept of sanctification found in Calvin's theological framework.[3] Like many other Confucian Koreans who converted to Christianity, he asserts that Jesus Christ, who obeyed the will of the heavenly Father unto death, was a human par excellence who most brilliantly disclosed the heavenly principle. He became the Way. Given this understanding, it makes sense why the Christian message about human salvation through Jesus Christ, as well as its emphasis on piety, were so well received by early Korean Christians. Pietism for them was nothing new. It is then no wonder that Korean Christians have engaged and continue to engage in rigorous religious practices for a pietistic living (*kyung-gun-han saeng-whal*) to do the will of heaven.[4]

Likewise, Korean American Christians are very interested in pietistic living. Pietistic living consists of not only daily individual practices such as prayer, Scripture reading, and hymn singing, but also communal practices such as tithing, feeding the poor, and making visits to the sick and shut-in. Most notably, Korean Christians practice dawn worship/prayer service. This practice has been carried over to the Korean American context. The number of Korean Americans who attend the dawn service every day before going to work is increasing. One Korean American likened this practice to tithing—one gives the first hour of one's day to God. Korean American Christians are definitely not Sunday Christians. In addition, many periodically engage in ascetic practices like fasting prayer to purify their minds in order that God's will may be revealed to them clearly.

WRESTLING WITH GOD THROUGH FASTING PRAYER (*KEUM-SIK KI-DO*)

She never left the temple but worshiped there with fasting and prayer night and day.

(Luke 2:37)

At daybreak, a woman walks into a room in the main building of the mountain prayer house. Her face has a flushed, feverish look. She looks excited and edgy. In a hoarse voice, she says that she has been praying all night, but somehow "cannot grasp the prayer line [ki-do-ju-ri jap-hee-ji an-ah-yo]."

Just as Jacob wrestled all night with an angel at the ford of the Jabbok, determined to receive a blessing, many Korean American Christians engage in a mighty wrestling with God. They do it when they are in need of a blessing or a clear revelation from God, often in times of crisis or when they are at a crossroads in need of the discernment of God's will. To make this wrestling a sincere effort that is acceptable to God, they fast and pray. If they can find time to get away, they will go to a special place like a prayer house (*ki-do-won*) to have time alone with God. This place is usually situated deep in the mountains, away from everyday surroundings.

Wherever they may be, Korean American Christians often engage in fasting prayer (*keum-sik ki-do*) for days, some even for as many as forty days, following the example of Jesus in the wilderness. Rather than silent meditation, they usually practice loud prayer, as in *tong-sung ki-do*. In prayer, they wrestle with God. Very often, their voices become hoarse because of prolonged loud prayer, usually all night. In very loud voices, they wail, confess, lament, cry out for help, and offer petitions and supplications. The loudness is perhaps a device used to dispel all impure thoughts, doubts, and other human desires. It is a device used to keep them awake, alert, since they often deprive themselves of sleep as well. They pray with all their strength. In order to provide privacy as well as the freedom to pray in a loud voice without disturbing others, many *ki-do-wons* have constructed prayer caves in their compound for individual pray-ers.

Fasting, of course, is an act of privilege for those who have food to fast from. It is not a choice for the starved and hungry. Yet refraining from food, however much or little one has, is never an easy choice. Fasting is a sincere, sometimes desperate act of faith made by Koreans and Korean Americans to enhance their spiritual alertness in prayer. Many of them believe that deprivation of the body helps them focus better spiritually.

Fasting as a practice gains more meaning in the Korean and Korean American context because it is born out of a cultural context known for its nurturing nature, especially by its love for feeding and communal feasting. In such a culture, fasting is not just denial of food from one's own body, but also an act of voluntary self-exclusion from the community. Still, the Christian community demands that the person on a fast do so without outward manifestation. This is in accordance with a stern teaching on fasting in the Bible that states, "'And whenever you fast, do not look dismal, like the hypocrites, for they disfigure their faces so as to show others that they are fasting. . . . But when you fast, put oil on your head and wash your face, so that your fasting may be seen not by others but by your Father who is in secret; and your Father who sees in secret will reward you'" (Matt. 6:16).

The practice of *keum-sik ki-do* is usually an individual practice engaged by one in need of discernment, protection from harm, blessings, and God's help. Many Korean American Christians will testify that everything is possible in God when one prays because they have witnessed the power of prayer in their lives. A minister planting a church without any financial resources may engage in fasting prayer to seek God's help. A mother whose son is sent to a battlefield may practice fasting prayer to ask God's protection of her son. A young woman who is pressured by her in-laws to bear a son may practice fasting prayer to have a son as Hannah did. An abused woman may practice fasting prayer to discern whether to leave her husband or not. A middle-aged man trying to decide whether to expand his business may choose to do fasting prayer to discern God's will. Two young people thinking about marriage may choose to engage in fasting prayer in search of God's will. This type of fasting prayer is often done in private, and often in prayer houses. Indeed, there are many prayer houses around big U.S. cities. Korean Americans come to these prayer houses hungry for God's will, willing to wrestle with God with all their strength and mind and heart.

However, *keum-sik ki-do* has also been practiced in Korea by groups of people and individuals as a nonviolent form of protest, and in such cases, it is practiced with public knowledge. For instance, for several years, theologically trained Korean women church employees and women seminarians engaged in fasting prayer for days immediately preceding the General Assembly of the Presbyterian Church of Korea (PCK) to demand women's ordination in the church.[5] Above their heads hung a banner that said, "Women's Ordination is God's Will. Women have waited half a century." This practice did not receive approval from many lay women leaders, also striving for their elder ordination, who chose more subtle ways of making their demands, like petitioning and waiting. They called the method too aggressive and incongruent with the Presbyterian sensibilities. Nonetheless, God's will prevailed and since 1996, PCK, the second largest Presbyterian denomination in Korea, has been ordaining women as elders and ministers.[6]

Fasting prayer in the Korean American context is very much an individual practice engaged in for personal needs and concerns. Although youth groups and/or other groups in the church occasionally take up fasting to help the needy with the money saved from skipping meals, Korean American Christians rarely come together for fasting prayer to raise concerns about bigger issues such as women's ordination.[7] One historical irony is that the PCK in the United States still does not ordain women despite the action taken by the General Assembly of PCK in Korea nine years ago. Although the issue has been coming to the floor of the assembly since the 1980s, there has not been any visible, organized effort to address the issue, such as a protest in the form of fasting prayer. Furthermore, the issue has not even surfaced in many other Korean American churches that belong to the Presbyterian Church in America (PCA), whose denominational polity does not ordain women. These churches are more aligned with the largest Presbyterian denomination in Korea, known as *Hapdong*, that has been scandalized recently by a remark made in the seminary chapel by its moderator regarding women's ordination. He said, "There is no chance that our denomination will ordain women as ministers. How dare that women think about standing in the pulpit wearing a diaper [euphemism for sanitary napkin but can have double meaning here]?"[8] This incident is popularly known as *ki-juh-ki sa-kwon* (the diaper incident).

The absence of fasting prayer for causes such as women's ordination in the United States is revealing. What is absent is not only the outward manifestation of communal protest. The Korean American practice of fasting prayer reveals very little or no active engagement of the world or issues of systemic injustice. Individually, Korean Americans may bring to God in prayer their concerns about injustice from which they and/or their immediate family members or friends are suffering. However, the petition in prayer is usually limited to the removal of the cause of pain for the individual or for strength to overcome the suffering. There is no outcry by the means of communal fasting prayer for God's justice to be done.

The practice of fasting prayer, of course, is not easy. It demands determination and dedication. When one considers that some Korean Americans fast for as many as forty days, one can only imagine what kind of discipline this practice requires. In this regard, one can see that fasting prayer entails, in essence, a deliberate act of saying yes and saying no.[9] Fasting is an act of saying a strong no to food and bodily comfort. In so doing, the practitioner says yes to something else, like the power of God as a source of strength. By saying no to ordinary circumstances, the practitioner says yes to a more focused relationship with God alone or to Christ's presence. This practice is then inherently a practice of saying no and saying yes, and it begs one to look deeper into the Korean American practice of saying no and saying yes. To what are Korean American practitioners of faith saying yes? To what are they saying no? How well does the Korean American practice of saying yes and saying no reflect the will of God?

SAYING YES AND SAYING NO

He has told you, O mortal, what is good;
and what does the LORD *require of you*
but to do justice, and to love kindness,
and to walk humbly with your God?
(Mic. 6:8)

"Do not judge, so that you may not be judged."
(Matt. 7:1)

Several years ago Dorothee Söelle, a German theologian, published a book entitled *Not Just Yes and Amen.* Inherent in the title is a critique on the church's ethos that has emphasized blind obedience, in other words, yes, to authority. In many Korean American churches, one often can hear the preacher say repeatedly the following words throughout the sermon: "If you believe, respond by saying Amen." The congregation's response is a resounding "Amen" in almost all instances. To understand just what it means to say yes or no in the Korean American context, one needs to examine more closely the Korean American practice of saying yes and saying no.

In her discussion of saying yes and no as a practice of faith, Shawn Copeland writes, "We must learn the practice of saying no to that which crowds God out and yes to a way of life that makes space for God."[10] Many Korean American Christians will resonate with that statement. So very often, one can hear in a public prayer offered in a worship service, "O Lord, forgive us for not working for spiritual matters that will live forever but working only for perishable food." Using Copeland's words, for Korean American Christians, what crowds God out are material concerns and what makes space for God is the spiritual search. Since the church serves as the spiritual center for Korean American Christians, most Korean American Christians do not hesitate to say yes to worship services, prayer meetings, district Bible study meetings, revival meetings, and hours given to other church activities. For many Korean American Christians one has to be at church to be faithful. Having been raised in a culture that takes very seriously the virtues of obligation, role appropriateness, and obedience, Korean American Christians are well prepared to do what has been laid out for them by the church. The biblical phrase "Moreover, it is required of stewards that they be found trustworthy" (1 Cor. 4:2) is a favorite passage quoted often by those who dedicate many hours to the church. Women in particular hold dedication services on a regular basis throughout the year to recommit themselves to their call to serve the church. Such practices definitely promote a culture of saying yes.

This culture makes it possible for Korean American Christians to accomplish many miracles, small and large. We can make things happen with short notice, even some things that might seem totally impossible. Our ability to respond to emergencies is impressive. The strength of saying yes can help Korean Americans overcome insurmountable obstacles. Many Korean American churches have been built because of the power of the practice of saying yes. In the Korean American context, some church members may go to the extent of refinancing their own homes in order to raise funds to build a church. Those without many financial resources may even wait to buy their own house until they have completed their obligation to building a church home. Indeed, a yes to many Korean American Christians means total commitment.

The shadow side of this yes-saying culture is that it makes it difficult to say no, and thus minority opinions can be easily ignored and silenced; it allows coerced collectivism to flourish. This is a concern when one considers that God often speaks through those who are on the margin. Such a culture also makes it easy for those in church leadership, especially the ministers, to abuse their power and expect too much from church members. Moreover, such a culture makes structural changes difficult. Korean American churches, for instance, still function as a dual-gender system where women and men have clearly defined roles. Age is also a big variable in the life of the Korean American faith community. For a people who have been trained to say yes to authority, it is difficult to imagine an alternate way of being, doing, and relating as a community of different genders, ages, and generations. There is usually a small decision-making body with a large body of followers who are expected to say yes to the decisions made. This does not mean that conflicts are absent in the Korean American situation, by any means. Schisms are frequent because a culture that stresses saying yes is not equipped with skills for conflict resolution.

The flip side of the Korean culture that stresses a strong yes is a strong no to everything that is not considered normative. Korean Americans have been trained to say no to anything that deviates from the behavioral patterns that have been set for them. Such a culture has engendered biblical literalism for many Protestant Christians. As a faithful people who try to live by set standards of behavior, they turn to the biblical texts that clearly spell out when to say yes and when to say no. Since this practice happens by internalizing imposed values, not much individual freedom is exercised, and it may deprive practitioners of faith opportunities for the discernment of the will of God in the true sense of the word. Such an approach has made Korean American Protestant Christians a rigid people who have difficulty dealing with differences and who are quick to judge.

To what then do Korean American Christians say no? As stated earlier, they say no to the works of the flesh that crowd God out:

> Live by the Spirit, I say, and do not gratify the desires of the flesh. For what the flesh desires is opposed to the Spirit, and what the Spirit desires is opposed to the flesh; . . . Now the works of the flesh are obvious: fornication, impurity, licentiousness, idolatry, sorcery, enmities, strife, jealousy, anger, quarrels, dissensions, factions, envy, drunkenness, carousing, and things like these. (Gal. 5:16–21a)

The focus of this practice of saying yes and saying no has been definitely on personal, individual morality. Such an emphasis has created pious individuals who have lived ethical lives on a personal level when measured by strict traditional standards of morality. One of these standards is in regard to the body because there seem to be few practices that honor the body in the Korean American context. Bound by a dualistic framework, the body has been understood to crowd God out. This anti-body stance of Christian practices has negatively contributed to spiritualizing many aspects of material matters. Pietism that denies the body and that is hostile to the imperfect human condition has contributed to a split of spirit and body. Its stress on moral perfection also created otherworldly Christians who do not say no to systemic injustices. Furthermore, the church's teaching that has emphasized the biblical passages, such as the Matthean passage that forbids people from judging others, has strengthened the orientation of disengagement of the world, leaving everything up to God. Unfortunately, the church has done little to teach Korean American Christians to practice saying no to injustices and yes to God's call to transform the world, as did prophets of the old who risked their lives by trying to discern and communicate the will of God to the people who did not want to hear it. Therefore, the Korean American faith community has not really supported contemporary prophets who have challenged unjust systems. Additionally, its practice of saying a strong no to anything considered un-Christian has contributed to creating a people intolerant to other religions.

As stated earlier, the Korean culture embodied by Korean Americans by and large dictates to its people that they live by the collective norms that govern their lives. Many Korean immigrants whose upbringing was influenced by Korean culture are not used to making conscious choices on an individual level on matters outside individual morality. This is largely due to their fundamental orientation in life. The Korean culture teaches that individuals are born into a network of relations, and therefore they can never be disparate individuals, apart from others. This complicates the decision-making process because people, rather than issues, become the focus. When facing choices, they are taught always to consider the implications of their actions on others, but often "others" include only those with whom they are closely identified, like the family and other social groupings.[11] Their decision-making process must first consider if their choice will contribute to the welfare of the networks to which they belong. On the one hand, this way of life can function as an antidote to the self-centeredness and individualism of modern society. On the other hand, this way of life tends toward collective egotism and exclusivity because of the tendency to consider only those who are in one's network.

In fact, Korean American churches contribute minimally to the welfare of the larger community and shy away from ecumenical efforts because church members tend to invest all of their energy and resources for the betterment of their individual churches.[12] One might think that language plays a big role in this isolationist tendency, but a similar tendency is easily observed in Korea where there is no language barrier. Given this orientation, it is difficult for Korean Americans to commit themselves to bigger circles of community beyond family and church. Bigger circles easily become too impersonal and difficult to identify with. The challenge for Korean Americans is the U.S. context, in which the majority culture does not share Korean American cultural norms. Furthermore, American culture emphasizes individualism and talks much about diversity. To meet these challenges, Korean Americans need to assess honestly their assumptions about norms and learn how and when to say yes and no. We must seek and do God's will in all dimensions of life, including the public life, because, as the saying goes, "The personal is political."

Korean Americans learned the lesson of the above phrase when our lives were negatively affected by what has been known as the Welfare "Deform" Act of 1996.[13] In the face of potential cutbacks in federally subsidized benefits due to their status as permanent residents, Korean Americans in large numbers applied for U.S. citizenship and gained citizen status. Nevertheless, this citizenship drive has not boosted the Korean American participation in the political process. In the November 2000 election, for instance, only thirteen percent of Korean American citizens voted. Hence, one needs to question why a strong yes to citizenship did not lead to a strong yes to exercising one's voting right. When one considers that voting entails essentially an act of saying yes and no, and that the majority of the Korean American population is affiliated with faith communities, one has to ask why Korean American people of faith do not take voting seriously as a faith practice.

However, a human dimension that needs to be considered in discussing the practice of saying yes and saying no has to do with the history of Korean people. Korean Americans are not exempted from the historical experience of oppression by global powers that colonized and divided Korea against the will of the Korean people. Many Korean Americans are refugees from the northern part of the Korean peninsula. Over the last twenty years, quite a few have made visits to North Korea to meet their families, risking their reputations and safety even in their faith communities because for such a long time Christianity has been strongly identified with anti-Communism.

The experience of ten million Koreans separated by the division is something that is worth considering, particularly at this juncture of Korean history. On August 15 to 19, 2000, fifty-five years after the division, one hundred South Koreans and one hundred North Koreans crossed the 38th parallel to meet with their family members on the other side. People around the world witnessed one of the most tragic human dramas unfold. Regardless of the reasons that separated the families, no one had expected their separation to last as long as it has. It must be remembered that no Korean made the decision to divide the country. It was done to them. The power to say yes and no to the future of their own country and land was taken from them.

In close to sixty years of separation, many things have happened. Many have died, everyone has grown older, and younger generations have been born. One person who was reunited with his family in the North for a few days in August 2000 was a man who fled to the South for fear of being killed, leaving his family behind. He waited for a day of unification, hoping to return to his family. When he lost hope after more than ten years of waiting, he married another woman in the South and had children by her. His son who had been left behind in the North said to him in exasperation, "I didn't want to say this to you. But, how could you leave Mom and us? Do you know how much suffering she has had to endure because you were not with us?" A son who was separated from his family in the South by joining the North Korean army came to see his father. When his aging father did not recognize him, he fell down to the floor and cried out, "Please forgive me. I have sinned against you." What should they or could they have done? When and how should they have said yes and no?

In discussing the practice of saying yes and no, one often assumes a situation where people have power and freedom to make decisions. The Korean situation lets us know that such is not always the case. When people are put in a life-and-death situation that is overcome with so many conflicting forces, they may not have the luxury to make an ethical choice of saying yes or no. In such situations, survival may become the only thing that matters. One thus needs to exercise caution in applying universal ethical values to every human situation. In practicing our faith, we must remember that God is merciful and that we must also be merciful in considering the choices made by others. As the Westminster Confession professes, God alone is the Lord of our conscience.

QUESTIONS FOR REFLECTION

1. Have you engaged in fasting prayer? If yes, what circumstances led you to consider fasting prayer? If not, what other practices do you engage in to discern the will of God?

2. Drawing on the discussions of the practices of fasting prayer (*keumsik ki-do*) and saying yes and saying no, think further about how you might want to engage in these practices by completing the following sentences. (Example: FAST from discontent; FEAST on gratitude.)

FAST from thoughts of illness; FEAST on _____.

FAST from anger; FEAST on _____.

FAST from _____; FEAST on phrases that affirm.

FAST from _____; FEAST on forgiveness.

FAST from problems that overwhelm; FEAST on _____.

FAST from _____; FEAST on _____.

3. Describe a situation when you experienced difficulty in making a decision. How did you say yes, and how did you say no? In what ways do you think your decision reflected the will of God?
4. Pietistic living has often been practiced within the bounds of individualized and privatized religion. Voting as a form of pietistic living challenges this notion. What other practices of saying yes and saying no help you to live out your faith in the public arena?
5. Sometimes one community's yes can be another community's no. Name some examples of your community's yes that can be experienced as no by other communities. How can one's yes be more accountable to another's no and vice versa?

Chapter 9

"Ricing" Community
The Practice of Hospitality

It is that time of the month. A major housecleaning and food shopping was done in advance. Women of the house are busy preparing the feast for their church's regional meeting. As members of the regional group gather, the aroma of succulent bul-go-gi *(thinly sliced beef marinated in Korean sauce),* kim-chee *(pickled Chinese cabbage), and rice fills the hosting house. With a brief exchange of greetings, well-wishes, and up-to-date news, the twenty or so assembled people start their monthly worship service while resisting the mouth-watering aroma of the feast to come afterwards. Jammed into a living room, the group begins worship with a prayer and continues on with hymn singing. Then it moves on to a Bible study led by a lay leader. During this time those assembled freely exchange insights and interpretations of the reading. The Bible study is followed by sharing mutual concerns, and the group ends the worship with a prayer. As the worship comes to its end, the group repositions itself to enjoy the much-anticipated fellowship by reassembling around* bap-sang, *the "table of rice." With men in the living room, women around the kitchen table, and children in the family room, the prepared dishes are served and consumed. And around these* bap-sangs *of abundant food, the community is strengthened, sustained, and renewed each and every month.*

Every month Korean American Christians are summoned to participate in *sok-whe/ku-yeuk-whe* (regional groups).[1] Such gatherings usually take place on Friday evening, Saturday, or Sunday evening. The main purpose of the monthly gathering is to provide a more intimate surrounding where faith can be shared and fellowship strengthened. The place of *sok-whe/ku-yeuk-whe* varies from time to time as different families in the region rotate to host the monthly meeting.

The head of the regional group usually takes the responsibility of calling and reminding church members who live in the area to attend. He or she may use the opportunity to invite members who have drifted away from the church as well as potential members in the area. Attendants are invited to participate not only in the worship and Bible study but also in helping to shape the community of hospitality—the *ricing* community. Hence, it is not unusual for the hosting family to extend the invitation to family friends and even other church members who live outside of the designated residential area. Such a family-friendly and neighbor-outreaching monthly gathering is often comprised of five to seven families.

While Korean American Christians are called to gather regularly to worship, study the Bible, and pray together as neighbors, these monthly gatherings are largely communities of "ricing." The term "ricing" as an active verb of "rice" denotes hospitality as the fundamental component of the Korean American Christian community. Since nurturing is the core practice of hospitality in the Korean/Korean American culture, and sharing resources is an important practice of hospitality in the Christian community, Korean American Christians' observance of the ricing community exemplifies the negotiated means by which they actively reproduce both ethnic and religious identities in the United States.

The portrayal of Korean American Christians' monthly gathering as the ricing community emphasizes two things: First, the host family spends days in preparation of the monthly meeting by cleaning, shopping, and cooking food to be served.[2] Also, most people spend much time and effort at the meeting presenting, serving, tasting, complimenting, and enjoying the abundantly prepared food. Moreover, along with rice, *kim-chee*, and *bul-go-gi* as the three "universal" main dishes at most Korean American gatherings, there are other fusion dishes that have no clear national/ethnic affiliations at these tables of ricing. Whether or not the host family introduces dishes that they are experimenting with as a culturally hyphenated people living in the United States, rice is the basic staple food in these gatherings. Indeed, it is not an exaggeration to say that the practice of feeding and feasting is to extend hospitality and to strengthen the ricing community for Korean American Christians. The second observation that can sustain the claim that these monthly meetings are largely communities of ricing is based on comparing the actual time spent in conducting the worship and Bible study and that spent enjoying the prepared food. The monthly meeting usually starts around seven in the evening and goes on until well past ten. During these three (or longer) hours, worship, including Bible study, often lasts less than an hour. During the rest of the time, people come together to exchange news of their family, business, and the church while enjoying the prepared food. By nurturing both the spirit and the body of everyone gathered, these gatherings function largely as ricing communities for Korean American Christians.

RICE IS HEAVEN

The Korean poet Kim Ji Ha declares that "rice is heaven" in one of his oft-cited poems. This outcry makes it explicit that heaven (the spiritual bliss) and rice (the staple food of the bodily bliss) are one and the same. Although the central role that food plays in shaping racial-ethnic and religious identities has been articulated in a number of studies,[3] there is something uniquely Korean American about equating rice with heaven. At the same time, there is something particularly Christian about how Korean Americans practice ricing in their faith communities. Juxtaposing the selected Korean and American cultures, and integrating selected histories of Christianity in Korea and Korean America, the rest of this chapter is divided into two subsections: the ricing community as a Korean American experience and the ricing community as a Christian practice.

THE KOREAN AMERICAN PRACTICE OF RICING

Eating together and thereby affirming a sense of community by sharing daily and bodily necessities is one of the most widespread activities in human societies. The often taken-for-granted activity of feeding and eating, however, is something that Koreans have had to constantly remember and struggle for throughout their nation's history. With ongoing conflicts and battles against neighbor countries' intrusions, Japanese colonialism, the Korean War, and the subsequent military dictatorial regimes, until very recently (South) Koreans have been preoccupied by the daily burden of satisfying their hunger. For example, the most common greeting among people until recently was said to be "Have you eaten?" The concern for satisfying one of the fundamental bodily needs, hunger, is also reflected in the Korean word for the "family" (*Sik-gu*). *Sik-gu* literally means the mouths to be fed in a household. Hence, members of the family are determined by and comprised of the people who share a pot of rice. The Korean notion of the family is, then, first and foremost a nurturing community of hospitality. And by exchanging the greeting of "Have you eaten?" Koreans sought to share well-wishes of others as extended family members.

Given this central role that eating and feeding play in Korean history, it is not surprising to hear many Korean proverbs that demonstrate the importance of food as essentially something to be shared. Take for example, the proverb "If you eat rice all alone by yourself, you will lose appetite." Another related adage, "*bap-madd* [appetite—which literally means 'the taste of rice'] is the same as *sal-madd* [the taste of life]." By equating the taste and the craving for rice with that of life, Koreans are reminding themselves of the communal responsibility to feed one another. To satisfy hunger is to live, and to eat rice together is to share life resources with others in the Korean culture.

There is another telling example of how Koreans experience eating together and feeding others as their most important cultural practice. Language is the key to the world of culture; thus Korean language opens up a world of Korean culture. It often amazes non-Korean speakers when they hear about the capacity of Korean language to denote extremely diverse and variant tastes and flavors of food. Just as Eskimos are endowed with many different words for articulating "snow" and its various consequences in their everyday life, Koreans are equipped with numerous ways of naming and expressing the taste of food. Along with the four main classes of differentiating tastes—sweet, sour/tart, salty, and hot/spicy, Korean language allows unlimited ways of expressing tastes, textures, and flavors of food. Take, for example, the different ways to express various spectrum of spiciness: *maep-da, mae-kom-ha-da, uhl-keun-ha-da, si-won-ha-da*, etc. Since language is the major means of cultural transmission, and "people are what they eat" (as some sociologists argue), the food-taste-friendly Korean language can tell much about who Koreans/Korean Americans are.

Integrating the selective aspects of the Korean culture and building the community of ricing take a special urgency and meaning in the United States as we come together as Korean Americans to remember who we once were, who we now are, and who we are called to become. Korean Americans at large live in a world dominated by political, economic, and cultural macroinstitutions. Subsequently Korean Americans long for the intimacy of smaller, familiar, and more directly personal communities. This tension between the estranged/alienated self and the familiar/communal self among Korean Americans is negotiated through the concrete experience of eating and sharing rice. That is why communal eating is a regular and frequent feature of Korean American gatherings. When Korean Americans come together to share rice, they are both reenacting the shared cultural memories and creating their own ethnic identities anew in the United States. Through the practice of ricing, Korean American Christians pass on their traditions from one generation to the next.

THE KOREAN AMERICAN CHRISTIAN
PRACTICE OF RICING

Day by day, as they spent much time together in the temple, they broke bread at home and ate their food with glad and generous hearts.

(Acts 2:46)

"My lord, if I find favor with you, do not pass by your servant. Let a little water be brought. . . . Let me bring a little bread, that you may refresh yourselves, and after that you may pass on.". . . And Abraham hastened into the tent to Sarah, and said, "Make ready quickly three measures of choice flour, knead it, and make cakes." Abraham ran to the herd, and took a calf,

tender and good, and gave it to the servant, who hastened to prepare it.
Then he took curds and milk and the calf that he had prepared, and set it
before them; and he stood by them under the tree while they ate.

(Gen. 18:3–8)

The story of Abraham's hospitality to strangers and God's blessing on Abraham is one of the most well remembered and emphasized stories for Korean American Christians. The story renders a powerful lesson on hospitality, and it has a special meaning for Korean American Christians. First-generation Korean immigrants especially feel a strong sense of affinity with the story because they know the meaning of hospitality from their lived experience of being strangers in a strange land. Moreover, since many first-generation Korean immigrants continue to experience cultural alienation and structural segregation from mainstream America, there is an urgent need to attend to their experiences of alienation and isolation. Given this context, the Korean American church often turns to the practice of ricing to help its faithful to recover their integrity, dignity, and sense of belonging as well as to attend to the strangers who come along the way.

As early Christians came together to share food with glad and generous hearts, most Korean American churches engage in the practice of ricing every Sunday during the fellowship hours that follow the worship service. Many actually serve a full lunch with rice and other scrumptious Korean dishes. By enacting and reminding people to share rice among God's family members (*sik-gu*) in the new land, the Korean American church practices and reinforces hospitality. This practice of ricing is actually a big draw, especially for lonely Koreans and Korean Americans, including the students from Korea who often are in the United States by themselves. As they come together around the ricing table to feed their bodies and spirits, their stories of sorrow and triumph are also shared, and a community is formed.

While the communal practice of ricing inside and outside of the church is important for sustaining Korean American Christian communities, ricing is also a deeply gendered phenomenon. Just as Abraham summoned his wife Sarah and other servants to prepare the food to be served, much of the food preparations and other labors related to experiencing the ricing community fall on the hands of Korean American women. Although the ricing community would not be possible without women's self-sacrificial services, their labor-intensive work is often rendered invisible and not recognized as a legitimate and significant form of ministry. At times, in order to prepare for the ricing table during the fellowship hour, Korean American women cannot even participate in the Sunday worship service. Furthermore, at least in some churches, in the name of preserving the Korean/Korean American culture, the church also reiterates the highly patriarchal and Confucian notion of serving the leadership, men, and the elderly first and foremost at the ricing table. Korean American women are relegated to serving others at their own homes, as well as at their church. Much needs to be changed in order for men and women to experience equal partnership in the ricing community.

It is intriguing to compare the experience of women at the ricing table with that at the communion table. Whereas women function as servers at the ricing table, they are the served at the communion table. Interestingly, the power dynamics that are in operation around the communion table are the reverse of what happens around the ricing table in the fellowship hall. At the communion table, the servers are people of authority in the faith community, and they are usually a male pastor and male elders. At the ricing table, the reverse is experienced. It is usually the people without authority, the women, who function as servers. In both cases, women are relegated to a secondary status. Much needs to be changed in order to experience the communion as an equal partnership.

The issue raised here demands attention, especially in light of the emergence of ministerial functions in the early church and their historical development. Acts 6 begins with a dispute that arose in the early church regarding the ministry of serving food. It is written, "'It is not right that we should neglect the word of God in order to wait on tables. Therefore, friends, select from among yourselves seven men of good standing, full of the Spirit and of wisdom, whom we may appoint to this task, while we, for our part, will devote ourselves to prayer and to serving the word'" (6:2b–4). So far, the separation of serving food and serving the Word appears to be simply a functional division. However, as the traditional reading of the story of Mary and Martha indicates, the church has traditionally treated serving the Word as the most important and recognized form of ministry while relegating serving food to women's work and not treating it as a legitimate form of ministry.[4] As women, we find a dilemma here. How can women sit at the Lord's feet to listen to God's Word as Mary did when serving food is defined as women's primary responsibility in church life?[5] Should some women serve food while other women listen to the Word of God? Who benefits from this teaching? Who does not?

While Korean American Christian women are often perceived as servants only, history testifies to their being faithful stewards. From the very beginning of the Christian history in Korea, there is much evidence that they contributed tremendously to building the churches and making the world more just and peaceful with the few resources they had. It is often said that "without women, Korean church buildings would not have been constructed." Since women did not have much access to financial resources, they turned to something they had: the rice. When faced with a national debt crisis in the early part of the Japanese colonial era, women carried out a movement to pay off the national debt using rice as a resource.[6] Women saved one spoonful of rice per family member at each meal. Although this movement was a secular movement, Christian women participated in large numbers. First-generation Korean Christian women also practiced *sung-mi*—which means rice dedicated out of devotion—by allocating and saving a few spoonfuls of rice at each meal time to contribute to supporting church staff and other causes, such as building churches.[7] During economically and politically unstable times, Korean Christian women were collecting rice together to feed the needy in their own communities, as well as to send rice to assist missionaries.[8] Throughout Korean history, women actively participated in the movement of *sung-mi* collection at the time of famine, drought, and other natural and national disasters. It is not surprising, then, to find both women Christians in Korea and Korean America taking active leadership roles in *sung-mi* collection to help feed the hungry North Korean children.

Indeed, rice is sacred in the context of Korean American faith communities. Just as the heaven/sky is shared among people, rice is also something that needs to be shared. And to this end, Korean American Christians actively practice the ricing community. The practice at regional meetings, in particular, has been proven to play a significant role in the overall ministry of the church in terms of community formation. The new challenge is, How big is this ricing table in the Korean American context? The author of Hebrews writes, "Let mutual love continue. Do not neglect to show hospitality to strangers, for by doing that some have entertained angels without knowing it" (Heb. 13:1–2). Who are the strangers that still have not been invited to the ricing table? What does their absence mean to the ricing community in the Korean American context?

QUESTIONS FOR REFLECTION

1. The Gospel of Matthew states, "For I was hungry and you gave me food, I was thirsty and you gave me something to drink, I was a stranger and you welcomed me, I was naked and you gave me clothing" (Matt. 25:35–36). What are your experiences of showing hospitality to strangers, therefore "entertaining angels" without knowing it?

2. In spite of emphasizing hospitality through eating together, there are many instances of schisms in the Korean American church community. How do you think eating together really enhances community formation?

3. Describe the current practice of communion in your own church community. What makes this practice uniquely Korean American? Discuss other possibilities of transforming the communion service to be more authentically Korean American. For example, what would be your reaction to serving rice instead of bread for communion?

4. While the practice of the ricing community invites everyone to the table, there seems to be a clear demarcation along the line of gender between those who serve and those who are served. Discuss how both women and men can mutually participate in serving and being

served. In what other ways can women practice hospitality besides providing rice?

5. Who are not invited to your table in your home? In your church? In your community? For instance, how would you practice the hospitality of ricing to someone infected with HIV?

Postscript

Three years after the completion of this manuscript, we gathered together again in Louisville, Kentucky, on the occasion of Unzu's house blessing. We flew in from New York and Atlanta and drove in from Chicago to celebrate and bless her new home. We arrived on a beautiful sunny day in April excited to see each other and to catch up with each other's lives. As is our custom, we discussed the menu for that weekend, way in advance, and we were looking forward to tasting each other's cooking. From barbeque ribs and fish, Korean spicy cold noodles, and cream scones to smoked salmon, cheeses, dried fruits, and crystallized ginger, we carefully planned the menu so that the eclectic variety of food did not clash. We gathered around the kitchen table cooking, eating, and drinking Korean rice wine. To bless the house, we created a ritual of "sharing home." As immigrants have carried pieces of home from their old land to make a new home in a new land, we brought pieces of our home to share, with wishes we have for this new home. A twenty-five-pound bag of rice, pasta, dried kelp, a music book, dried mushrooms and mountain vegetables that we brought from our trip to North Korea, and other items were laid out on the table with lit candles and incense. Given the importance that "home" as a physical reality and a guiding metaphor was for us as immigrants, we spoke of how these items created home for us. We spoke of "ricing" our homes and our sisterhood. We shared memories of creating home in new spaces and new lands. We recollected our parents' attempts to create home for us. We blessed Unzu's home as a place of safety, contentment, hospitality, and love. To close the ritual, we sang our favorite hymns.

As we reflect on our ritual, we are struck by how our "searching for home" has come a full circle. Even as we recollect our parents' stories[1] as refugees from northern Korea before the division of the Korean land, we have more recently become involved in going back "home," to North Korea. Three members of our group traveled to North Korea last summer in search of a home and family members left behind. The dried mushrooms and mountain vegetables signified our connection to our "go-hyang," the homes of our ancestors. Our searching for home has led us to embark on our next project documenting Korean American women's contribution towards peaceful reunification of Korea. It will be done through the lens of women's leadership—identifying different styles of Korean American leadership through interviews of several generations of Korean American women.

Finally, just as our mothers made attempts to create home for us in this new land, it is our responsibility to make home for our daughters, the next generation of women who are in search of a home. Through studying and researching the embodied self-image of younger Korean American women, we wish to document ways that their bodies embody "home." We ask ourselves, "How do our daughters sing the Lord's song in this land?" Singing, after all, is an embodied practice.

To our mothers—who sang to us the songs of their unfailing faith, at times off-key and with jumbled lyrics—and to our daughters—who challenge us to sing new and different songs, with different rhythms that make our ears uncomfortable—we dedicate this book with great love and affection.

Endnotes

Introduction

1. Dorothy Bass and Craig Dykstra, "Life Abundant: A Theological Understanding of Christian Practices" in *Practicing Our Faith: A Way of Life for a Searching People*, ed. Dorothy C. Bass (San Francisco: Jossey-Bass, 1997), 9.
2. The twelve practices in Dorothy Bass's book are: honoring the body, hospitality, household economics, saying yes and saying no, keeping sabbath, testimony, discernment, shaping communities, forgiveness, healing, dying well, and singing our lives.
3. Bass, 8–10.
4. This term "ritual genesis" is borrowed from Prof. Hope Leichter of Teachers College, Columbia University. It is a probing of "how the ritual began."

Chapter 1: A Social History

1. This chapter is a revision of the previously published work, along with reprints of sections from Jung Ha Kim's "Cartography of Korean American Protestant Faith Communities in the United States," in *Religions in Asian America: Building Faith Communities*, ed. Pyong Gap Min and Jung Ha Kim (Walnut Creek, Calif.: AltaMira Press, 2002).

2. Raymond Brady Williams, *Christian Pluralism in the United States: The Indian Immigrant Experience* (New York: Cambridge University Press, 1996), 3–4.

3. R. Stephen Warner, "The Korean American Immigrant Churches as Case and Model," in *Pilgrims and Missionaries from a Different Shore: Korean Americans and Their Religions*, ed. Ho-Youn Kwon, Kwang Chung Kim, and R. Stephen Warner (University Park: Pennsylvania State University Press, 2001), 1.

4. Ibid., 20.

5. For further reading on these topics, see Won Moo Hurh and Kwang Chung Kim, *Korean Immigrants in America: A Structural Analysis of Ethnic Confinement and Adhesive Adaptation* (Rutherford, N.J.: Fairleigh Dickinson University Press, 1984); Kwang Chung Kim and Shin Kim, "The Ethnic Roles of Korean Immigrant Churches in the U.S.," in Kwon, Kim, and Warner, *Pilgrims and Missionaries;* Karen Chai, "Inter-ethnic Diversity: Korean Buddhists and Protestants in Greater Boston" and "Beyond 'Strictness' to Distinctiveness: Generational Transition in Korean Protestant Churches," in Kwon, Kim, and Warner, *Pilgrims and Missionaries*; Ai Ra Kim, *Women Struggling for New Life: The Role of Religion in the Cultural Passage from Korea to America* (Albany: State University of New York Press, 1996); Jung Ha Kim, *Bridge-makers and Cross-bearers: Korean American Women and the Church* (Atlanta: Scholars Press, 1997); Jung Young Lee, *Marginality: The Key to Multicultural Theology* (Minneapolis: Fortress Press, 1995); Pyong Gap Min, *Caught in the Middle: Korean Merchants in America's Multiethnic Cities* (Berkeley: University of California Press, 1996); and Kyeyoung Park, *The Korean American Dream: Immigrants and Small Business in New York City* (Ithaca, N.Y.: Cornell University Press, 1997).

6. Bass, *Practicing Our Faith*, 5.

7. Nancy T. Ammerman, *Congregation and Community* (New Brunswick, N.J.: Rutgers University Press, 1997), 47.

8. Anne S. Brown and David D. Hall, "Family Strategies and Religious Practices: Baptism and the Lord's Supper in Early New England," in *Lived Religion in America: Toward a History of Practice*, ed. David D. Hall (Princeton, N.J.: Princeton University Press, 1997), 62.

9. Alasdaire MacIntyre, "The Virtues, the Unity of a Human Life, and the Concept of a Tradition," in *Memory, Identity, Community: The Idea of Narrative in Human Sciences*, ed. Lewis I. Hinchman and Sandra K. Hinchman (Albany: State University of New York Press, 1977), 259.

10. Gary Y. Okihiro, Rony Alquizola, and K. Scott Wong, eds., *Privileging Positions: The Sites of Asian American Studies* (Pullman: Washington State University Press, 1995), 93.

11. Ibid., 94.

12. This type of sociological grasping of the interplay between "history and biography and the relations between the two within society" is called "sociological imagination." See C. Wright Mills, *The Sociological Imagination* (New York: Grove Press, 1961), 6.

13. Finke and Stark, *The Churching of America, 1976–1990: Winners and Losers in Our Religious Economy* (New Brunswick, N.J.: Rutgers University Press, 1992), 6.

14. David Yoo, *New Spiritual Homes: Religion and Asian Americans* (Honolulu: University of Hawaii Press, 1999), 10.

15. Sucheng Chan, *Asian Americans: An Interpretive History* (Boston: Twayne, 1991); Lucie Ching and Edna Bonacich, eds., *Labor Immigration Under Capi-*

talism: Asian Workers in the United States before World War II (Berkeley: University of California Press, 1984); and Harry Kitano, *Race Relations*, 5th ed. (Upper Saddle River, N.J.: Prentice Hall, 1997).

16. Rev. H. N. Allen was not the first Protestant missionary to Korea but rather the first missionary from the United States. After spending some years in China first, Rev. C. Gutzlaff from Germany was the first Protestant missionary ever to enter into Korea, in 1832. For further information on both Allen and Gutzlaff's work in Korea, see Yong-Suk Oh's *Hankook Kidokkyo ei Konan (The Persecution of Christianity in Korea)* (Seoul: Institute of Korean Christian Cultural Studies, 1985).

17. Kwang-Mok Lee, *Kewahaki Kwangsuhjibang kwa Kiddokkyo (The Kwansuh Region and [the Spread] of Christianity during the "Open Policy")* (Seoul: Institute of Korean Christian Cultural Studies, 1983).

18. Jung Ha Kim, *Bridge-makers and Cross-bearers*; and Wayne Patterson, *The Korean Frontier in America: Immigration to Hawaii, 1896–1910* (Honolulu: University of Hawaii Press, 1988).

19. Nancy Abelmann and John Lie, *Blue Dreams: Korean Americans and the Los Angeles Riots* (Cambridge, Mass.: Harvard University Press, 1995); and Kyeyoung Park, *The Korean American Dream*.

20. Lee, *Kewhaki Kwansuhjibang*; and Oh, *Hankook Kiddokkyo*.

21. The Korea-America Treaty was signed in 1882. Citing the original study of Wayne Patterson's *The Korean Frontier in America: Immigration to Hawaii, 1896–1910*, both Nancy Abelmann and John Lie's and Kyeyoung Park's works documented some "twenty-odd ginseng merchants" (Abelmann and Lie, *Blue Dreams*, 52), along with another handful of Korean students and diplomats.

22. Bong-Youn Choy, *Koreans in America* (Chicago: Nelson-Hall, 1979); Warren Kim, *Koreans in America* (Seoul: Po Chin Cha, 1971); and Kitano, *Race Relations*.

23. Kim, *Koreans in America*, 10.

24. The first group of contracted laborers from Japan entered into Hawaii in 1868. They were comprised of 141 men, 6 women, and a child (Jere Kahahashi Takahashi, *Nisei/Sansei: Shifting Japanese American Identities and Politics* [Philadelphia: Temple University Press, 1997], 15–16).

25. Kitano and Daniels, *Asian Americans*, 169.

26. L. Houchins and C-S Houchins, "The Korean Experiences in America, 1903–1924," in *Asian American*, ed. N. Hundley (Santa Barbara, Calif.: Clio Press, 1976), 135, and Kitano, *Race Relations*, 269.

27. Chan, *Asian Americans*; Kitano, *Race Relations*; and Patterson, *The Korean Frontier in America*.

28. W. Peterson, "Concept of Ethnicity," in *Harvard Encyclopedia of American Ethnic Groups* (Cambridge, Mass.: Harvard University Press, 1988); and Chae-Kun Yu, "The Correlates of Cultural Assimilation of Korean Immigrants in the U.S." in *The Korean Diaspora*, ed. Hyung-chan Kim (Santa Barbara, Calif.: ABC-Clio Inc., 1977), 36.

29. Rev. G. H. Jones was a missionary sent out by the United Methodists in the United States. He was also known by his adopted Korean name, Won-shi Oh. Along with his main parish, the Youngdong Church in Inchon, Rev. Jones also had close connections with other "branch" churches in Seoul and Pusan.

30. San Oak Cho, "A Study of Korean American Churches and Their Growth in the U.S." (unpublished Ph.D. diss., Fuller Theological Seminary, Pasadena, California, 1984); and Lee, *Kewahaki Kwangsuhjibang*, 1983.

31. Cho, "A Study of Korean American Churches."

32. Kyeyoung Park cites that 1,100 picture brides came to the United States from Korea during this historical period (based on the *Annual Report* [1995] of the U.S. Immigration and Naturalization Service); cited in *The Korean American Dream* (1998).

33. Elaine H. Kim and Eui-Young Yu, eds., *East to America: Korean American Life Stories* (New York: New Press, 1997), 369.

34. Ibid.

35. Kitano, *Race Relations*, 269.

36. Shirley Geok-Lin Lim, "Immigration and Diaspora," in *An Interethnic Companion to Asian American Literature*, ed. King-Kok Cheung (New York: Cambridge University Press, 1997), 296.

37. Won Moo Hurh, "How They Fared in American Homes: A Follow-up Study of Korean American Children," in *Children Today* 6 (1967): 102; also mentioned in Hurh and Kim, *Korean Immigrants in America.*

38. Won Moo Hurh, "Marginal Children of War: An Exploratory Study of Korean-American Children," in *International Journal of Sociology of Family* 2 (1972): 16; and Ministry of Health and Social Affairs, *A Handbook of Korea* (Seoul: Korean Overseas Information Services, 1967).

39. Velina Hasu Houston, "The Past Melts the Future: A Cultural Essay," *Amerasia Journal* 17 (1991): 79.

40. Cheryl Crabb, "Families Celebrate Korean Kid's Culture," *Atlanta Constitution* (September 13, 1999): D4.

41. Some Asian wives and children of U.S. servicemen entered as nonquota immigrants under the War Bride Act of 1945. But the McCarran Walter Act of 1952 is important for understanding Korean wives of U.S. servicemen. Further, unlike Chinese brides who mostly married co-ethnics, Korean wives of G.I.s "more often than not married non-Asian men," (see Espiritu, *Asian American Women and Men* [Thousand Oaks, Calif.: SAGE Publications, 1997], 56).

42. Chan, *Asian Americans,* 140.

43. Bok-L. Kim, "Casework with Japanese and Korean Wives of Koreans," in *Social Case Work* 53 (1972): 272–79; and Pong Gap Min's *Asian Americans: Contemporary Trends and Issues* (Thousand Oaks, Calif.: SAGE Publications, 1995).

44. Cited in Kim and Yu, *East to America,* 1.

45. Ibid., 10.

46. Ibid., 11.

47. The dating of 1988/1992 as a dividing point between viewing Korean American communities mostly as "immigrant" communities or "transnational" communities is again none other than my own attempt to reconstruct and make better sense of the history of Korean American religions. Having said this, I see the years 1988 and 1992 as the two most significant eventful years for understanding contemporary Korean American experiences. For instance, if South Korea's hosting of the Olympic Games in Seoul in 1988 was the key event that impeded Korean Americans from coming to terms with their experiences of "cognitive dissonance," the "*Sa-I-Ku,*" otherwise known as the L.A. uprising, in 1992 was a wake-up call for Korean Americans to reassess their complacent dreaming of the "American Dream." By probing the significance of these two historical events, I argue that Korean Americans at large have experienced the transition from being predominantly an immigrant community to a more conscious transnational community.

48. Hyun Y. Kang, "Re-membering Home," in *Dangerous Women: Gender and Korean Nationalism*, ed. Elaine H. Kim and Chungmo Choi (New York: Routledge & Kegan Paul, 1998).

49. Ibid., 250.

50. Lim, "Immigration and Diaspora," 297, 292.

51. U.S. Bureau of the Census, *1990 Census of the Population: Asian and Pacific Islanders in the United States* (Washington, D.C.: Government Printing Office, 1993). Other statistical data from the U.S. Census for 1970, 1980, and 1990 were cited in Kitano, *Race Relations,* Min, *Asian Americans,* and Park, *The Korean American Dream.* By year 2000, there were 1.23 million Koreans, including Koreans who are part Korean, and mixed race. See *The New Face of Asian Pacific America: Numbers, Diversity and Change in the 21st Century,* eds. Eric Lai and Dennis Arguelles (San Francisco: Asian Week, 2004).

52. These data released by the U.S. Census are inevitably conservative. Underdocumented and undocumented Korean immigrants are not included in these figures.

53. Kang, "Remembering Home," 250.

54. While there are churches that serve particular class, occupation, and gender groups in South Korea, no Korean American church claims to serve exclusively a particular people of specific social categories. For example, there are at least two well-established Protestant churches in South Korea where the majority adherents are *yeo-nai-in* (literally, "popular entertainers" or "artists"), such as actors/actresses, singers, etc.; and the Women's Church was also formed in the late 1980s by feminist women theologians who critiqued the masculine perspectives and articulations in *Ming Jung* theology (often translated as "commoners," "the oppressed," and "grass-roots people"). Most founders of the Women's Church are educated in Bible colleges and/or seminaries in the United States.

55. Michael Omi and Howard Winant, *Racial Formation in the United States: From the 1960s to the 1980s* (New York: Routledge & Kegan Paul, 1986).

56. Peter Kwong, "Asian American Studies Needs Class Analysis," in *Privileging Positions: The Sites of Asian American Studies*, ed. Okihiro et al. (Pullman: Washington State University Press, 1995), 74.

57. Ibid., 75.

58. Ibid., 76.

59. An in-depth analysis of Korean American labor participation and its impact on family life has been conducted. Pyong Gap Min, for example, documented an unusually high percentage of self-employed Korean merchants in the greater Atlanta area: "An Exploratory Study of Kin Ties Among Korean Immigrant Families in Atlanta," in *Journal of Comparative Family Studies* 15 (1984): 75–86. Also see Min and Charlie Jaret, "Ethnic Business Enterprises: The Case of Korean Small Business in Atlanta," *Sociology of Social Research* 69 (1985): 412–35.

60. Sang Hyun Lee, "Called to Pilgrims: Toward an Asian-American Theology From the Korean Immigrant Perspective," a revised paper of an essay published in *The Korean Immigrants In America*, ed. Sang Hyun Lee and Byongshu Kim (Montclair, N.J.: Association of Korean Christian Scholars, 1986).

61. The feminization of Korean American Christian faith communities is well documented in works such as Hurh and Kim's "Religious Participation of Korean Immigrants in the U.S."; Ai Ra Kim's *Women Struggling for a New Life*; and Jung Ha Kim's *Bridge-makers and Cross-bearers*.

62. Chan (*Asian Americans,* 146) further specified the seven preferences for immigrants under the 1965 Immigration Act: 1) U.S. citizens' unmarried children

under age twenty-one; 2) permanent residents' spouses and unmarried children; 3) professionals, scientists, and some artists; 4) U.S. citizens' married children over age twenty-one; 5) U.S. citizens' siblings; 6) skilled and unskilled laborers who can be placed in short supply in the U.S.; and 7) refugees. These categories of preference are also cited in Espiritu (1997).

63. Espiritu Yen Le, *Asian American Panethnicity: Bridging Institutions and Identities* (Philadelphia: Temple University Press, 1993), 63.

64. Chan, *Asian Americans*; Kim, *Bridge-makers and Cross-bearers*; Lowe, *Immigrant Acts: On Asian American Cultural Politics* (Durham, N.C.: Duke University Press) and Min, *Asian Americans*.

65. The labor force of both garment and microelectronic industries constitute about 80 to 90 percent of female workers (Espiritu, *Asian American Women and Men*; Lowe, *Immigrant Acts*). As a largely nonunion industry, "as many as half of these assembly workers are recent immigrants from the Philippines, Vietnam, [South] Korea, and South Asia" (Espiritu, 77).

66. Chan, *Asian Americans*; Kim, "The Labor of Compassion: Voices of 'Churched' Korean American Women," *Amerasia Journal* 22 (1996): 93–105; and Takaki, *Strangers from a Different Shore*.

67. Linda Y. C. Lim, "Capitalism, Imperialism, and Patriarchy: The Dilemma of Third-World Women in Multinational Factories," in *Women, Men, and International Division of Labor*, ed. Nash and Fernandez-Kelly (Albany: State University of New York Press, 1983), 78.

68. Cited in Espiritu, *Asian American Women and Men*, 76.

69. Ai Ra Kim, *Women Struggling for a New Life*, and Jung Ha Kim, *Bridge-makers and Cross-bearers*.

70. The term "reverse immigration" refers to the more widely used notion of "return migration" in social science. In the context of Korean American community, however, "immigration" often refers to the one-way movement from their homeland to another country, such as the United States. While "immigration" connotes more of a permanent move and the status of mind, "migration" connotes continuous movement between the homeland and the other country. Although other terms, such as "twice migrant" or "return migrant," can be useful, "reverse immigrant" is the term that most closely describes what Korean Americans are experiencing.

71. John J. Macionis, *Sociology*, 7th ed. (Upper Saddle River, N.J.: Prentice Hall, 1999), 295.

72. *Korean Journal* (February 1989): 19–25; *Southeast News* (December 1988) 18–24; and *Southeast News* (October 30–November 4, 1989).

73. The U.S. Immigration and Naturalization Service counted the entry of 35,849 Korean immigrants into the United States in 1987; 34,703 in 1988; 34,222 in 1989; 32,301 in 1990; and 26,516 in 1991. The drastic decline of the number of Korean immigrants is recorded from 1992 to 1995: 19,359 in 1992, 18,026 in 1993, and 10,799 in 1994. The same data are also cited in Min, *Asian Americans* and K. Park, *The Korean American Dream*.

74. This estimate is released by "Radio Seoul" (a Korean language radio station in the United States) and was also printed in *Korea Times Los Angeles*, English ed., May 11, 1992. The same data and more detailed table of categories of Korean-owned businesses were also documented in Min, *Asian Americans*.

75. *Korea Times*, May 11, 1992; and *Southeast News*, May 19, 1992.

76. The term "*Sa-I-Ku*" refers to the L.A. riot/uprising. The literal meaning of "*Sa-I-Ku*" is "4-2-9" in Korean. It commemorates the significance of April 29 (1992) in the formation of the Korean American consciousness. Korean Ameri-

cans' reluctance to name what had happened from April 29 to May 2, 1992, in Los Angeles as "riot," "uprising," or "rebellion" is significant in and of itself. The date of this historical incident is thus included in the "*Sa-I-Ku.*"

77. The U.S. Bureau of the Census, 1990.

78. Timothy P. Fong, *The Contemporary Asian American Experience: Beyond the Model Minority* (Upper Saddle River, N.J.: Prentice Hall, 1998), 41.

79. David K. Kim, "Becoming: Korean Americans, Faith, and Identity—Observations on an Emerging Culture," Master of Divinity thesis, Harvard Divinity School, 1993; and Antony W. Alumkal, "Being Korean, Being Christian: Particularism and Universalism in a Second Generation Congregation," in Kwon, Kim, and Warner, *Pilgrims and Missionaries.*

80. Minho Song, "Towards the Successful Movement of the English-Speaking Ministry Within the Korean Immigrant Churches," a paper presented at Katalyst, March 21–24, 1994; cited in Karen J. Chai, "Competing for the Second Generation: English-Language Ministry at a Korean Protestant Church," in *Gatherings in Diaspora*, ed. Stephen Warner and Wittner (1998), 295–332; and Helen Lee, "Silent Exodus," *Christianity Today* (August 12, 1996): 51–52.

81. Chai, "Competing for the Second Generation," and Kelly Chong, "What It Means To Be Christian: The Role of Religion in the Construction of Ethnic Identity and Boundary among Second Generation Korean Americans," *Sociology of Religion* (1998): 58.

82. Mannheim, "The Problem of Generations," in *Essays on the Sociology of Knowledge by Karl Mannheim*, ed. Paul Keeskemeti (London: Routledge & Kegan Paul, 1928 [1963]),127.

83. Kim and Yu, *East to America*, 174.

84. Donald C. Goellnicht, "Blurring Boundaries: Asian American Literature as Theory," in *An Interethnic Companion to Asian American Literature*, ed. King-kok Cheung (Cambridge: Cambridge University Press, 1997), 355.

85. T. Minh-ha Trinh, *Women, Native, Other: Writing Postcoloniality and Feminism* (Bloomington: Indiana University Press, 1989), 84.

Chapter 2: This Is the Day

1. Referred to as either *sae-byuk ki-do-whe* (dawn prayer meeting) or *sae-byuk ye-bae* (dawn worship service), this prayer meeting/worship service follows a simple unwritten liturgy although its major emphasis is on prayer. Instead of a homily, some ministers choose to give a short Scripture exposition, turning it more into a Bible study.

2. If an observer were to follow the weekly rhythm of a typical Korean American faith community, it would look like this: Daily dawn prayer meeting to start the day; Sunday service, followed by either an evening service or a regional group worship service; Wednesday evening midweek service; Friday evening Bible study; and, at home, a daily family worship service. Throughout the year, there would be revival meetings, women's dedication services, and youth worship services as needed.

3. Jung Young Lee, *Korean Preaching: An Interpretation* (Nashville: Abingdon Press, 1997), 62–63. For a different historical explanation of the genesis of this practice, see the discussion of *tong-sung ki-do* as lamentation in chapter 4: "Fervent Prayer."

4. Some scholars equate *ki* with the Holy Spirit or *ruach* in Hebrew and *pneuma* in Greek. See Peter K. H. Lee, "Dancing, *Ch'i* and the Holy Spirit," in *Frontiers*

of Asian Christian Theology: Emerging Trends, ed. R.S. Sugirtharajah (Maryknoll, N.Y.: Orbis Books, 1994), 65–79.

5. Craig Dykstra and Dorothy Bass, "Times of Yearning, Practices of Faith" in *Practicing Our Faith: A Way of Life for a Searching People*, ed. Dorothy C. Bass (San Francisco: Jossey-Bass, 1997), 7.

6. Dorothy C. Bass, *Receiving the Day: Christian Practices for Opening the Gift of Time* (San Francisco: Jossey-Bass, 2000), 63–71.

Chapter 3: Let Everything That Has Breath, Sing!

1. Jung Young Lee, *Korean Preaching* (Nashville: Abingdon Press, 1997), 53.

2. Amateur male members of the choir are often chosen to lead the choir even when there are female members who have professional training in music.

3. This hymnal is published in two versions. One version has 183 gospel songs as an appendix. The gospel songs are sung usually in preparation of the worship, but seldom during the worship service.

4. Publication of this bilingual hymnal was initiated by the Steering Committee of the National Korean Presbyterian Council of the United Presbyterian Church in the United States of America and made possible by the support of the United Presbyterian Church U.S.A. and the Presbyterian Church in Korea. The membership of the Korean-English Hymnbook Publication Commission consisted of prominent first-generation Presbyterian ministers and church musicians currently engaged in ministry in the United States, and they included those who were not part of the UPCUSA. See Preface of the *Korean-English Hymnbook* (Southfield, Mich.: Korean-English Hymnbook Publication Commission, 1978), 1.

5. The selection of the hymns included in this hymnal is quite different from that of the Korean hymnal. According to its preface, this hymnal includes twenty-two hymns that are not found in the Korean hymnal published in 1967 that was in current use. Among the twenty-two, ten are English translations of the hymns written by Koreans, and the other twelve are Korean translations of the hymns written in English. In addition, the hymnal includes the national anthems of Canada, Republic of Korea (South), and the United States. The commission writes in its preface that the inclusion of these hymns was motivated by its desire "to enrich the Christian life through exchange of the experiences of both the East and West." See *Korean-English Hymnal*, ed. Korean Hymnal Society (Seoul: Word of Life Press, 1984).

6. In the perspective of the Korean Christian community in South Korea, the emergence of many Korean immigrant churches in English-speaking countries such as the United States and Canada was an evidence of growth of the Korean church and therefore a cause to celebrate. Thus, the Korean church leadership felt a responsibility to respond to the emerging need of bilingualism, and the publication of the bilingual hymnal was its response.

7. Chun Jin Lee gives the following as the organizational structure of the majority of the hymns included in the Korean hymnal:

- 75 hymns are the ones recommended by the World Council of Churches.
- 56 hymns are the ones recommended for hymn education by the Southern Baptist Church in the United States. Twenty hymns are German hymns.
- 17 hymns have a Korean either as their composer or lyricist.
- 269 hymns are American gospel songs.

For more discussion, see Chun Jin Lee, "History of the Korean Church Hymnals and Korean Hymn (3)," in *Sungsil Moonwha* (Seoul: Sungsil Worship Education Cultural Center, no. 29, 2001–2002), 78–92.

8. Chun Jin Lee, "The History of Korean Church Hymnals and the Korean Hymn (1)," *Sungsil Moonwha* (Seoul: Sungsil Worship Education Cultural Center, no. 25, 2000–2001), 106.

9. Lee, "History of Korean Church Hymnals (3)," 81.

10. For example, the *Presbyterian Hymnal*, the hymnbook of the Presbyterian Church (U.S.A.), includes a hymn that uses the most popular Korean folk song "*Arirang*" as its melody.

11. Lee, "History of Korean Hymnals (1)," 101–102.

12. *Come, Let Us Worship: The Korean-English Presbyterian Hymnal and Service Book* (Louisville, Ky.: Geneva Press, 2001). The United Methodist Church's bilingual hymnal contains the same selection of 392 hymns chosen by the hymnal committee that represented both UMC and PC(USA). However, the two versions have different liturgical resources, each rooted in its unique liturgical tradition. One additional difference is "The Psalms and Canticles" section found in the Presbyterian version. This section includes fifty psalms whose format provides for responsive reading and sung refrains. Each psalm has a refrain that has a musical score attached to it, and it is composed using the Korean musical modality.

13. Lee, *Korean Preaching*, 54.

14. Saliers, "Singing Our Lives," in *Practicing Our Faith*, 185.

15. The emotional complex of resentment and sorrow that results from repeated experiences of suffering is called *han* by Koreans. *Han* is also the term used to describe the experiences Koreans have suffered collectively throughout history. Chung Hyun Kyung has called *han* the Korean people's "root experiences" or "collective consciousness" in her article "*Han-pu-ri*: Doing Theology from Korean Women's Perspective" in *The Ecumenical Review* 40 (January 1988): 30. For more discussion of *han*, see the "Community at the Well" chapter.

16. *Han-pu-ri* literally means to untangle *han*. *Han-pu-ri* therefore is an act engaged in to resolve conflicts, release tension, and bring healing. Korean shamans, most of whom are female, are often called the priestesses of *han-pu-ri*.

Chapter 4: Fervent Prayer

1. The 1965 Immigration Act allowed certain skilled professionals, e.g., doctors and nurses, to immigrate into the United States to fill the lack of labor in these areas. Many women came here as nurses who became the main "rice-winners" in many Korean American families.

2. *Han* is defined as "a sense of unresolved resentment against injustice suffered; a sense of helplessness because of the overwhelming odds against onself, a feeling of total abandonment ("Why hast thou forsaken me?"), a feeling of acute pain or sorrow in one's guts and bowels making the whole body writhe and wiggle, and an obstinate urge to take 'revenge' and to right the wrong" in Young-Hak Hyun's "Minjung and Suffering Servant and Hope," unpublished paper presented at Union Theological Seminary, New York, 13 April 1982. Cited in Andrew Sung Park, *Racial Conflict and Healing: An Asian-American Theological Perspective* (Maryknoll, N.Y.: Orbis Books, 1996), 19.

3. For another account of the ritual genesis of dawn prayer, see the discussion of dawn prayer in chapter 2.

Chapter 5: Resourcing the Life Circle

1. Tae Joon Kim, "*Jeol* (Bow), *Che-sa* (Rite of Veneration), Christianity," *Hyang Lin* 24 (Fall 1997): 7–8. Kim writes that the current practice of commemorating ancestors commonly known as *che-sa* originated from the rite of *che-sa* that Koreans practiced long before Confucianism became an organizing principle of the Korean society. It was a nationwide ritual to give thanks to the heaven, offer a petition for another year of prosperity, and foster communal solidarity. Confucianism, adopted as a political ideology of the Yi dynasty (1392–1910), changed the nature of the practice dramatically by differentiating *che-sa* into class-specific rites. According to the system of *che-sa* developed by Chinese Confucianists, *che-sa* for the heaven became a rite practiced only by the Chinese emperor. The rite of *che-sa* for commoners became strictly localized in the family, and the object of *che-sa* became ancestors, instead of heaven.

2. Throughout its history that spans thousands of years, Koreans have had diverse perspectives on life and death as reflected in indigenous faith practices such as shamanism, Taoism, Buddhism, and Confucianism. Ancestor veneration as a concept and practice has varied depending on the perspective of the people on life and death. In the beginning of the Yi dynasty (1392–1910), this became a highly contested issue between Confucianists and Buddhists. See Kim, "*Jeol* (Bow), *Che-sa* (Rite of Veneration), Christianity," 8–9.

3. In the perspective of neo-Confucianists on life and death, regeneration and ancestor veneration became the most important moral imperatives in order to continue the patrilineal family lineage. A very rigid patriarchal organization of the society emerged during this era, and *che-sa* became highly male-centered and ancestor-centered. The death of a woman, child, or someone who met a tragic death was not considered worthy of commemoration through *che-sa*.

4. *In* (*jen* in Chinese) is considered a cardinal virtue in the Confucian thought, but many different interpretations have been given by philosophers for the concept. Love, benevolence, and humanity are some of the English translations given for the term. For the Confucian scholar Tu Wei-Ming, *in/jen* signifies the fullest manifestation of humanness. For more discussion, see Tu Wei-Ming, *Centrality and Commonality* (Albany: State University of New York Press, 1989), 50–52, 57–58, 61, 102.

5. Heup Young Kim, "John Calvin and Yi T'oegye: Astonishing Similarities in Radical Differences," unpublished paper presented at the 1999 American Academy of Religion meeting, 5.

6. Tu, *Centrality and Commonality*, 45.

7. On June 13, 2000, the heads of the two divided Koreas met in Pyung Yang, the capital city of the Democratic People's Republic of Korea, for the first time since the division. Since then, there have been many exciting and hopeful developments. In celebration of August 15 (Korean liberation from Japanese), one hundred South Koreans went to Pyung Yang to meet their family members in the North, and one hundred North Koreans came to Seoul to meet their family members in the South. Another such encounter took place in December 2000.

8. He was notified a few days before he left for North Korea that the information given to him about his mother had been incorrect. She was no longer living. Korea was liberated from the Japanese on August 15, 1945.

9. In fact, one theme that was brought forth consistently in almost every family union was the ancestor veneration rite (*che-sa*). At least two families set a ritual table for their deceased parents, and the aging son in each family who was

reunited briefly with their separated families in the South bowed to his parents, asking for forgiveness for his failure to practice filial duties (*pul-hyo*).

10. When Catholicism was introduced to Korea in the eighteenth century, Rome had declared ancestor veneration unbiblical, and therefore early converts to Roman Catholicism refused to practice the ancestor veneration rite (*che-sa*). Rome's position since then has become more tolerant, especially since the Vatican II in 1965. The Catholic Church in Korea has embraced the traditional Korean ritual calendar of mourning and conducts the mass for the dead on the third, seventh, and thirtieth day after the death. It also holds a special mass on All Saints' Day. The Protestant church has been more consistent in its opposition to the ancestor veneration rite (*che-sa*) in its theological stance. However, many divergent views exist as it continues to struggle with issues of culture and gospel. For more information, see Myung Hyuk Kim, "Historical Understanding on the Ancestor Veneration Rite [author's translation]" in *The Korean Church and Che-sa* [author's translation], ed. Jong Yoon Lee (Seoul: Emmaus Publishing Co., 1985), 55–78.

11. Bowing is a custom commonly practiced to show respect in the Korean cultural context. Thus, it is not at all surprising that bowing is an integral element of the ritual process of the four rites of passage mentioned before. Bowing to the living was accepted by the Western Christian church as an acceptable custom; however, bowing to the dead has been interpreted as idol worship.

12. The practice of ancestor veneration ritual in the Protestant Christian context is today a hotly debated issue for some churches in Korea that take seriously the issue of cultural integrity. One church declared that "ancestor veneration ritual (*che-sa*) is an age-old ritual practice for people of Korean ancestry that needs to be embraced as a Christian practice . . . *che-sa* that was once judged as idol worship is not idol worship and it is not any different than a memorial service in the Western tradition." Quoted from Tae Joon Kim, "*Jeol* (Bow), *Che-sa* (Rite of Veneration), Christianity," 2. This issue addresses the issue of Christianity and ancestor veneration as a special issue and even presents the ancestor veneration ritual liturgy developed by Kyung Dong Church in Korea as a model. See 5–20 of the same issue for more discussion.

13. Anthony Wilhelm, *Christ Among Us: A Modern Presentation of the Catholic Faith for Adults*, 5th rev. ed. (San Francisco: HarperSanFrancisco, 1990), 444.

Chapter 6: Bearing Wisdom

1. Chung-Yung xx:11, translated by Wing-tsit Chan in *Chinese Philosophy* (1973); cited by Tu, *Centrality and Commonality*, 58.

2. Tu, *Centrality and Commonality*, 48–50.

3. The term "elder" applies to the position of lay leader elected by the congregation to serve in its governing body in the Presbyterian system. Although the United Methodist Church has a different polity that confers the status of "elder" to ordained clergy, Korean American churches in the United Methodist Church have a position of "elder" for lay leadership.

4. Historically it has been a common practice for Korean American churches in the Presbyterian tradition to confer the status of "*kwon-sa*" to the women of mature age who are married to "elders." In the changing Korean American church context, where some women have begun to enter the ranks of "elders" that used to be exclusively male, a common trend seems to be to elect to the position of an "elder" only those women who are either single or married to

men who are not "elders" and to continue to confer the position of *"kwon-sa"* to the women who are married to "elders." On the one hand, the practice allows the church governing body to avoid concentration of power that may happen by having both husband and wife serve on the session, which is usually given as a rationale to justify such practice. On the other hand, it takes away the right of a woman to be elected for leadership in her own right as an individual member of a congregation and limits married women's access to positions of leadership with decision-making power, thus creating an arbitrary division in church women's leadership—some as *"kwon-sas"* and some as "elders." This practice illustrates the difficulty involved in adopting the Western democratic system based on individual rights for people like Koreans for whom "self-in-relation" is the understanding that is most basic to organizing a society.

5. In his discussion of politics in Confucian perspective, Tu writes that "the goal of politics is not only to attain law and order in a society but also to establish a fiduciary community through moral persuasion. The function of politics then is centered on ethical education." Tu, *Centrality and Commonality,* 48.

Chapter 7: Gathering at the Well

1. This idea was first articulated by Yu Sun Kim, a Korean American United Methodist pastor.

2. As discussed in chapter 2, Koreans have their own "living water" (*sang-soo*) that springs from the depth of the mountain and is filled with the spirit of the mountaion. Can Korean American Christians drink from both sources of the "living water"?

3. Shin, Eui Hang, and Hyung Park, "An Analysis of Causes of Schism in Ethnic Churches: The Case of Korean-American Churches," *Sociological Analysis: A Journal of the Sociology of Religion,* 49, no. 3.

4. Andrew Sung Park in his book *Racial Conflict and Healing: An Asian-American Theological Perspective* ([Maryknoll, N.Y.: Orbis Books, 1996], 19) quotes from Young-Hak Hyun's "*Minjung* and Suffering Servant and Hope" (unpublished paper presented at Union Theological Seminary, New York, 13 April 1982).

5. The following dialogue illustrates how a shaman intercedes on behalf of a man in South Korea who has asked her to perform *kut* for his father, who fled to the south with him and died in South Korea, and his mother in the north, from whom he was separated at the time of Korean division.

(The shaman summons t'he spirit of the mother in the north.)

Mother: The war [the Korean War] has separated us. I am glad to find you alive. I lived alone in the north [i.e., North Korea], waiting for your father and you to return to me. But the 38th parallel line has stopped our reunion. I died in my prime time without seeing you again. My son, your mommy was beautiful, and so is my daughter-in-law [*myuneuri*]. She looks after me.

Shaman: (charges the mother spirit) Grandmother, give them blessings. What shall we give you?

Mother: (turns to her son) Today I will meet your father and we will go together. I have these unresolved sorrows and grudges in my heart. (She takes a soft persimmon from the altar.) Have this soft persimmon. There are a lot of persimmons in the north. . . . How would I have known that I would die before I saw your father again?

Quoted from Soon-Hwa, Sun, "Women, Religion, and Power: A Comparative Study of Korean Shamans and Women Ministers" (Ph.D. diss., Graduate School of Drew University, October 1991), 127.

6. Su Pak Drummond, "A Woman at the Well: Drawing the Ancestral Waters; A Korean American Woman's Reflection" in *Religious Education*, 93, no. 3 (1998): 389.

7. A similar tension existed when Buddhism and later Confucianism became the state religion in Korea. Over the years, however, neither Buddhism nor Confucianism was able to root out completely shamanic practices from the religious life of the Koreans, especially the commoners and women. In fact, there is a lot of intermingling of religious practices of different religions in the Korean context. Shamanism has incorporated elements from Buddhism, Taoism, and Confucianism; and Buddhism has incorporated elements from shamanism, Confucianism, and Taoism.

8. David Kwang-sun Suh, *The Korean Minjung in Christ* (Hong Kong: Christian Conference of Asia, 1991), 111.

Chapter 8: Thy Will Be Done

1. Yun Dong-Ju, "Prelude" in *Korea's Golden Poems,* translated by Chang-soo Ko (Seoul: Hanlin Publishing House, 1998), 54.

2. See Heup Young Kim, "John Calvin and Yi T'oegye: Astonishing Similarities in Radical Differences," unpublished paper presented at the annual meeting of the American Academy of Religion in 1999, 15.

3. Ibid., 15–16.

4. In the previous chapter, "Gathering at the Well," there is a discussion about Korean shamanism and Christianity. Both the Confucianism and shamanism nurtured the psyche of the Korean people: Confucianism as the rational, male (*yang*) principle and shamanism as creative, chaotic, female (*yin*) principle. In Jungian terms, it can be said that Korean shamanism played the compensatory function of the unconscious against the prevailing patriarchal rational consciousness. See Bou-Yong Rhi, "Psychological Aspects of Korean Shamanism," *Contemporary Philosophy: A New Survey* 7 (1970): 253–68.

5. Women's ordination was first discussed in the Korean Presbyterian church context as early as 1934. The Presbyterian faith community has gone through schisms over the later years. Among the three largest Presbyterian denominations, the Presbyterian Church in the Republic of Korea, the smallest of the three, was the first one to start ordaining women in 1974.

6. The Presbyterian Church in Korea (PCK) has established itself as a Korean Presbyterian denomination in the United States. Quite a few U.S. Presbyterian churches belong to the PCK rather than the Presbyterian Church (U.S.A.) or the Presbyterian Church in America (PCA). PC(USA) has a sister relationship with PCK in the United States.

7. Occasionally, Korean American activists have used fasting as a way of registering their protest against something, such as the Welfare Reform Act in 1996.

8. *Ki-ppeun So-sik (Good News), Journal of Association of Christian Women Minjung* 105 (Spring 2004): 73. The remark was made on Nov. 12, 2003, and it

has galvanized women across denominations against sexism in the church. "Diaper" is euphemism for feminine sanitary napkin.

9. See M. Shawn Copeland, "Saying Yes and Saying No," in *Practicing Our Faith*, ed. Dorothy C. Bass (San Francisco: Jossey-Bass, 1997), 59.

10. Ibid., 60.

11. Connections that are central to the way a Korean organizes his or her networks include blood connection, school connection, and regional connection. For men, the military connection is considered very important.

12. Most of the missionary activities carried out by Korean American churches take place outside the United States, like Mexico, countries in the continent of Africa, or Russia. Much less attention is paid to the problems that exist in their immediate context.

13. The so-called Welfare Reform Act was passed by Congress in 1996. In the context of Asian America, this Act prohibited legally documented permanent residents from accessing and benefiting from various federal programs. The immediate aftermath of the Welfare Reform Act resulted in a rapid increase in the number of Asian American elderly applying for U.S. citizenship. For example, during 1997, the number of Korean American elderly who applied for U.S. citizenship increased from a little over 1,000 per year in previous years to 35,000 in greater Atlanta alone.

Chapter 9: "Ricing" Community

1. A Korean congregation is divided into smaller parishes, and these parishes are called *sok-whe* (a Methodist term) or *ku-yeuk-whe* (a Presbyterian term used liberally by other denominations as well). These groups are usually geographically based, but alternate small groups based on their divergent needs, such as language, have been emerging in recent years.

2. Variations exist in terms of food preparation. Some regional groups do potluck and expect the host family to prepare only the rice, *kim-chee*, and a meat dish. In some other groups, the host family does all of the food preparation, since these meetings take place on a rotation basis anyway. Some groups limit the number of dishes to practice good stewardship.

3. See, for example, Peter Goldsmith's *When I Rise Cryin' Holy: African-American Denominationalism on the Georgia Coast* (New York: AMS Press, 1989) for the centrality of food as a religious expression in an African American Pentecostal community; and Dodson and Gilkes's "'There's nothing like church food'— Food and the U.S. Afro-Christian Tradition: Re-membering Community and Feeding the Embodied S/spirit(s)," *Journal of the American Academy of Religion* 63 (1995): 519–38.

4. On this issue of division of the one ministry into two, the biblical scholar Elizabeth Schüssler Fiorenza writes, "The division . . . into the ministry at table and the ministry of the word probably reflects a later practice of the Christian missionary movement, while the subordination of one to the other and the ascription of these ministries to certain groups clearly express Luke's own situation." Moreover, according to Fiorenza, "serving at table" as found in Acts 6:2 most likely meant service at the "table of the Lord," meaning the eucharistic table. From *In Memory of Her* (New York: Crossroad, 1985), 165.

5. Nowhere in the text (Luke 10:38–42) is it written that Martha was busy in the kitchen preparing food; there is no mention of a meal. Therefore, Fiorenza con-

tends that if Martha was busy serving at the table, she most likely was involved in preparing the eucharistic table as a leader of a house church.

6. For more information, see Woojung Lee, *Han-kook Ki-dok-kyo Yo-song Baek-nyun-eui Bal-ja-chwi* (Seoul: Minjung Publishers, 1985), 146–50.

7. *Sung-mi* was a Christian appropriation of an already existing practice in Korea. Practitioners of *chun-do-kyo,* an indigenous Korean religion also known as *Dong-hak,* made a regular offering of rice to Choe Je-u, who founded the religious movement in 1860.

8. Woojung Lee, *Han-kook Ki-dok-kyo Yo-song,* 79.

Postscript

1. Jung Ha's, Unzu's, and Su Yon's parents are from northern Korean prior to the division of the Korean peninsula. They were refugees to south before the Korean War.

Resources

Practices

Bass, Dorothy C., ed. *Practicing Our Faith: A Way of Life for a Searching People.* San Francisco: Jossey-Bass, 1997. Translated into Korean by Huh Jung Gap (Paul J. Huh) as *Il-sang-eul Tong-han Mid-eum Hyuk-myung.* Seoul: Jeyoung Communications Publishing House, 2004.

Bass, Dorothy C. *Receiving the Day: Christian Practices for Opening the Gift of Time.* San Francisco: Jossey-Bass, 2000.

Bass, Dorothy C., and Don C. Richter, eds. *Way to Live: Christian Practices for Teens.* Nashville: Upper Room Books, 2002.

Long, Thomas G. *Testimony: Talking Ourselves into Being Christian.* San Francisco: Jossey-Bass, 2004.

Paulsell, Stephanie. *Honoring the Body: Meditation on a Christian Practice.* San Francisco: Jossey-Bass, 2002.

Saliers, Donald, and Saliers, Emily. *A Song to Sing, A Life to Live: Reflections on Music as Spiritual Practice.* San Francisco: Jossey-Bass, 2004.

Van Engen, John, ed. *Educating People of Faith: Exploring the History of Jewish and Christian Communities.* Grand Rapids: Wm. B. Eerdmans Publishing Co., 2004.

Volf, Miroslav, and Dorothy C. Bass, eds. *Practicing Theology: Beliefs and Practices in Christian Life.* Grand Rapids: Wm. B. Eerdmans Publishing Co., 2002.

Theology and Religion in Korean/Asian America

Chung, David. *Syncretism: The Religious Context of Christian Beginnings in Korea.* Albany, N.Y.: SUNY Press, 2001.

Chung, Ruth, and David Yoo, eds. *Sacred Spaces: Religion and Spirituality in Korean America.* New York: New York University Press, forthcoming.

Hertig, Young Lee. *Cultural Tug of War: The Korean Immigrant Family and Church in Transition.* Nashville: Abingdon Press, 2002.

Iwamura, Jane Naomi, and Paul Spickard, eds. *Revealing the Sacred in Asian and Pacific America.* New York: Routledge & Kegan Paul, 2003.

Kwon, Ho-Youn, Kwang Chung Kim, and Stephen Warner, eds. *Pilgrims and Missionaries from a Different Shore: Korean Americans and Their Religions.* University Park: Pennsylvania State University Press, 2001.

Lee, Inn Sook, and Timothy Son, eds. *Asian Americans and Christian Ministry.* Seoul: Voice Publishing Co., 1999.

Lee, Jung Young. *The Trinity in Asian Perspective.* Nashville: Abingdon Press, 1996.

———. *Korean Preaching: An Interpretation.* Nashville: Abingdon Press, 1997.

Lee, Sang Hyun, and John V. Moore, eds. *Korean American Ministry* (expanded English edition). Louisville, Ky.: General Assembly Council, Presbyterian Church (U.S.A.), 1987.

Liew, Tat-siong Benny, ed. *The Bible in Asian America,* special edition, *Semeia* 90/91, Atlanta: Society of Biblical Literature, 2002.

Matsuoka, Fumitaka. *Out of Silence: Emerging Themes in Asian American Churches.* Cleveland: United Church Press, 1995.

Matsuoka, Fumitaka, and Fernandez, Eleazar S., eds. *Realizing the America of Our Hearts: Theological Voices of Asian Americans.* St. Louis: Chalice Press, 2003.

Min, Pyong Gap, and Jung Ha Kim, eds. *Religions in Asian America: Building Faith Communities.* Walnut Creek, Calif.: Alta Mira Press, 2002.

Park, Andrew Sung. *Racial Conflict and Healing: An Asian American Theological Perspective.* Maryknoll, N.Y.: Orbis Books, 1996.

———. *The Wounded Heart of God: The Asian Concept of Han and the Christian Doctrine of Sin.* Nashville: Abingdon Press, 1993.

Phan, Peter C., and Jung Young Lee, eds. *Journeys at the Margin: Toward Autobiographical Theology in Asian-American Perspective.* Collegeville, Tenn.: Liturgical Press, 1999.

Thangaraj, M. Thomas. "Theological Education in the United States: A View from the Periphery." *Theological Education* 28, no. 2 (1992): 8–20.

Yoo, David. *New Spiritual Homes: Religion and Asian Americans.* Honolulu: University of Hawaii Press, 1999.

Yu, Chai Shin. *Korea and Christianity.* Seoul: Korean Scholar Press, 1996.

Korean/Asian American Women, Theology, and Religion

Journal of Asian and Asian American Theology. Special issue on "Asian and Asian American Women's Voices." Claremont, Calif.: Center for Asian Studies, vol. 2, no. 1 (Summer 1997).

Brock, Nakashima Rita, Jung Ha Kim, Kwok Pui-lan, Nantawan Boonprasat Lewis, Greer Anne Wenh-In Ng, Seung Ai Yang, and Gale A. Yee. *Developing Teaching Materials and Instructional Strategies for Teaching Asian And Asian American/Canadian Women's Theologies in North America.* Boston: The Women's Theological Center, 1999.

Chai, Alice Yun. "The Struggle of Asian and Asian American Women toward a Total Liberation: A Korean Methodist Woman's Vocational Journey." In *Spirituality and Social Responsibility: Vocational Vision of Women in the United Methodist Tradition*, edited by Rosemary Skinner Keller. Nashville: Abingdon Press, 1993.

Kim, Ai Ra. *Women Struggling for a New Life: The Role of Religion in the Cultural Passage from Korea to America.* Albany, N.Y.: SUNY Press, 1996.

Kim, Grace Ji-Sun. *The Grace of Sophia: A Korean North American Women's Christology.* Cleveland: Pilgrim Press, 2002.

Kim, Jung Ha. *Bridge-makers and Cross-bearers: Korean American Women and the Church.* New York: Oxford University Press, 1997.

Kim, Jung Ha, and Rosetta R. Ross. *The Status of Racial-ethnic Minority Clergywomen in the United Methodist Church.* Nashville: Board of Ordained Ministry, 2003.

Ng, G. A. Wenh-In, ed. *Our Roots, Our Lives: Glimpses of Faith and Life from Black and Asian Canadian Women.* Toronto: United Church Publishing House, 2003.

Southard, Naomi P. F. "Recovery and Rediscovered Images: Spiritual Resources for Asian American Women." In *Feminist Theology from the Third World*, edited by Ursula King. Maryknoll, N.Y.: Orbis Books, 1994.

Women's Concerns Unit, Christian Conference of Asia, eds. *Reading the Bible as Asian Women.* Singapore: Christian Conference of Asia, 1986.

Yee, Gale A. *Poor Banished Children of Eve: Women as Evil in the Hebrew Bible.* Minneapolis: Fortress Press, 2003.

Korean/Asian American Experience and History

Abelmann, Nancy, and John Lie. *Blue Dreams: Korean Americans and the Los Angeles Riots.* Cambridge, Mass.: Harvard University Press, 1995.

Aguilar-San Juan, Karin, ed. *The State of Asian America: Activism and Resistance in 1990s.* Boston: South End Press, 1994.

Ancheta, Angelo N. *Race, Rights and the Asian American Experience.* New Brunswick, N.J.: Rutgers University Press, 1998.

Chan, Sucheng. *Asian Americans: An Interpretive History.* Boston: Twayne Publishers, 1991.

Hall, Patricia Wong and Victor H. Hwang, eds. *Anti-Asian Violence in North America: Asian American and Asian Canadian Reflections on Hate, Healing, and Resistance.* Walnut Creek, Calif.: Alta Mira Press, 2001.

Hong, Maria, ed. *Growing Up Asian American.* New York: Avon Books, 1993.

Kim, Claire Jean. *Bitter Fruit: The Politics of Black-Korean Conflict in New York City.* New Haven, Conn.: Yale University Press, 2000.

Kim, Elaine H., and Eui-Young Yu, eds. *East to America: Korean American Life Stories.* New York: Pew Press, 1997.

Kim, Kwang Chung. *Koreans in the Hood: Conflict with African Americans.* Baltimore: Johns Hopkins University Press, 1999.

Kitano, Harry H. L., and Roger Daniels. *Asian Americans: Emerging Minorities.* Englewood Cliffs, N.J.: Prentice Hall, 1988.

Liem, Ramsay. "History, Trauma, and Identity: The Legacy of the Korean War for Korean Americans." *Amerasia Journal* 29, no. 3 (2003–2004): 111–29.

Liu, Eric. *The Accidental Asian: Notes of a Native Speaker.* New York: Random House, 1998.

Min, Pyong Gap. *Changing Conflicts: Korean Immigrant Families in New York.* Boston: Allyn & Bacon, 1998.

———. *Caught in the Middle: Korean Merchants in American Multiethnic Cities.* Berkeley: University of California Press, 1997.

Osajima, Keith Hiroshi. "Breaking the Silence: Race and the Educational Experiences of Asian American College Students." In *Readings on Equal Education.* Vol. 2, edited by Michele Foster. New York: AMS Press, Inc., 1991.

Palumbo-Liu, David. *Asian/American: Historical Crossings of a Radical Frontier*. Stanford, Calif.: Stanford University Press, 1999.

Park, Kyeyoung. *The Korean American Dream: Immigrants and Small Business in New York*. Ithaca, N.Y.: Cornell University Press, 1997.

Park, Kyu Young. *Korean Americans in Chicago*. Charleston, S.C.: Arcadia Publishing, 2003.

Pembertson, Delores, and Young Pai. *Improving Communication: Handbook for Korean American Families*. Nashville: Cokesbury, 1992.

Suzuki, Bob H. "Asian Americans as the 'Model Minority': Outdoing Whites? Or Media Hype?" *Change* (November/December 1989): 13–19.

Takaki, Ronald. *Strangers from a Different Shore: A History of Asian Americans*. New York: Penguin Books, 1989.

Vo, Linda Trinh, and Bonus, Rick, eds. *Contemporary Asian American Communities*. Philadelphia: Temple University Press, 2002.

Woo, Deborah. *Glass Ceilings and Asian Americans: The New Face of Workplace Barriers*. Walnut Creek, Calif.: Alta Mira Press, 2000.

Xing, Jun. *Asian America through the Lens: History, Representations, and Identity*. Walnut Creek, Calif.: Alta Mira Press, 1998.

Yuh, Ji-Yeon. *Beyond the Shadow of Camptown: Korean Military Brides in America*. New York: New York University Press, 2002.

Zia, Helen. *Asian American Dreams: The Emergence of an American People*. New York: Farrar, Straus & Giroux, 2000.

Gender in Korean/Asian America

Chow, Claire S. *Leaving Deep Water: The Lives of Asian American Women at the Crossroads of Two Cultures*. New York: Dutton, 1998.

Eng, Phoebe. *Warrior Lessons: An Asian American Woman's Journey into Power*. New York: Simon & Schuster, 2000.

Hane, Shirley, and Gail M. Nomura. *Asian/Pacific Islander American Women: A Historical Anthology*. New York: New York University Press, 2003.

Hernández, Daisy, and Rehman Bushra, eds. *Colonize This! Young Women of Color on Today's Feminism*. New York: Seal Press, 2002.

Ho, Wendy. *In Her Mother's House: The Politics of Asian American Mother-Daughter Writing*. Walnut Creek, Calif.: AltaMira Press, 1999.

Kang, Hyun Yi, Norma Alarcon, and Lisa Lowe. *Writing Self, Writing Nation: A Collection of Essays on DICTEE by Theresa Hak Kyung Cha*. Berkeley, Calif.: Third Woman Press, 1994.

Kang, Laura Hyun Yi. *Compositional Subjects: Enfiguring Asian/American Women*. Durham, N.C.: Duke University Press, 2002.

Kim, Elaine H., and Chungmoo Choi, eds. *Dangerous Women: Gender and Korean Nationalism*. New York: Routledge & Kegan Paul, 1998.

Lee, Inn Sook, ed. *Korean American Women: Toward Self-Realization*. Montclair, N.J.: Association of Korean Christian Scholars in North America, Inc., 1985.

Nam, Vickie, ed. *Yell-Oh Girls! Emerging Voices Explore Culture, Identity, and Growing Up Asian American*. New York: Quill, 2001.

Oh, Angela E. *Open: One Woman's Journey*. Los Angeles: UCLA Asian American Studies Center Press, 2002.

Shah, Sonia, ed. *Dragon Ladies: Asian American Feminists Breathe Fire*. Boston: Southend Press, 1997.

Trinh, T. Minh-ha. *Women, Nation, Other: Writing Postcoloniality and Feminism*. Bloomington: Indiana University Press, 1989.

Yuh, Ji-Yeon. *Beyond the Shadow of Camptown: Korean Military Brides in America*. New York: New York University Press, 2002.

History of Korea/Korea-U.S. Relations

Chandra, Vipin. *Imperialism, Resistance and Reform in Late Nineteenth Century Korea*. Berkeley, Calif.: Institute of East Asian Studies, 1988.

Chol, Seong Ok. "Prostitution on U.S. Military Bases." *Korea Report* (January–February, 1989): 10–12.

Cummings, Bruce. *Korea's Place in the Sun*. New York: W. W. Norton, 1997.

Cummings, Bruce, and Jon Halliday. *Korea: The Unknown War*. New York: Viking/Penguin, 1988.

Harrison, Selig S. *Korean Endgame: A Strategy for Reunification and U.S. Disengagement*. Princeton, N.J.: Princeton University Press, 2002.

Moon, Katharine H.S. *Sex Among Allies*. New York: Columbia University Press, 1997.

Sturdevant, Saundra Pollock, and Stoltzfus, Brenda. *Let the Good Times Roll: Prostitution and the U.S. Military in Asia*. New York: New Press, 1992.

Yuh, Ji-Yeon. *Beyond the Shadow of Camptown: Korean Military Brides in America*. New York: New York University Press, 2002.

Selected Novels and Memoirs of Korean American Experiences

Choi, Susan. *The Foreign Student*. New York: HarperPerennial, 1999.

Hwang, Caroline. *In Full Bloom*. New York: Dutton, 2003.

Kang, K. Connie. *Home Was the Land of Morning Calm: A Saga of a Korean-American Family*. Reading, Mass.: Addison-Wesley Publishing Co., 1995.

Keller, Nora Okja. *Comfort Woman*. New York: Penguin Books, 1997.

———. *Fox Girl*. New York: Penguin Books, 2002.

Kim, Charles. *Subkorean*. Philadelphia: Xlibris, 2003.

Kim, Elizabeth. *Ten Thousand Sorrows: The Extraordinary Journey of a Korean War Orphan*. New York: Doubleday, 2000.

Kim, Helen. *The Long Season of Rain*. New York: Henry Holt, 1996.

Kim, Patti. *A Cab Called Reliable*. New York: St. Martin's Press, 1997.

Kim, Ronyoung. *Clay Walls*. Seattle: University of Washington Press, 1987.

Kim, Suki. *The Interpreter*. New York: Picador, 2003.

Lee, Chang-rae. *Native Speaker*. New York: Riverhead Books, 1995.

———. *A Gesture Life*. New York: Riverhead Books, 1999.

———. *Aloft*. New York: Riverhead Books, 2004.

Lee, Helie. *Still Life with Rice*. New York: Touchstone, 1997.

Na, An. *A Step from Heaven*. New York: Speak, 2001.

Paik, Mary. *Quiet Odyssey*. Seattle: University of Washington Press, 1990.

Stout, Mira. *One Thousand Chestnut Trees*. New York: Riverhead Books, 1998.

Robinson, Katy. *Single Square Picture: A Korean Adoptee's Search for Her Roots*. New York: Berkley Trade, 2002.